The EVIDENCE for
Heaven

To Dawn
May this book be
a special blessing
to you!

[signature]

The EVIDENCE for Heaven

David W. Balsiger
and
Charles E. Sellier

Bridge-Logos

Gainesville, Florida 32614

Bridge-Logos
Gainesville, FL 32614 USA

Printed in the United States of America.

Library of Congress Catalog Card Number: pending
International Standard Book Number 0-88270-823-6

Unless otherwise noted, all Scripture notations are
taken from the King James Version (KJV) of the Bible.

G1.316.m505.35250

"Well done, thou good and faithful servant; enter thou into the joy of thy Lord"
(Matthew 25:21 KJV).

CONTENTS

Part 3
From the Halls of Science: Research & Proof

Acknowledgement

We want to express our appreciation to Joe Meier for his research and editorial assistance on this book. We'd also like to express our deep appreciation to Bev Browning for her editorial services and untiring effort to help us bring this book to fruition. And finally, we'd like to thank Marsha Rano and Ina Moore for their counsel and editing assistance on this book. We are in awe of what our research uncovered that went into this book and the TV special of the same title, as well as the secular TV version entitled *The Search for Heaven*.

Dedication

This book is dedicated to Barbara Petty, who was a researcher on numerous TV shows and books for us. Barbara went to Heaven to be with the Lord after completing her part of the research on this Heaven book.

PREFACE

Is there a spiritual realm where the soul resides upon our death? In short—Is there a heaven? These questions are as old as humanity and as new as the latest scientific research. To Christian believers, the answers to these questions are a foregone conclusion. But, for believers and non-believers alike, the topic of life after death in a place called heaven raises even more questions. Where is heaven? What will heaven be like? Will we continue to learn in heaven or will we instantly know everything? Will life beyond the one we are experiencing here and now be free from pain and suffering? Will our bodies be different in heaven? Will we be married in heaven? If we can find the answers to these and other questions it will unravel many of the mysteries that have haunted humankind since the beginning of time.

Is there now scientific evidence that heaven really does exist? If we find the borders of heaven, do we also discover the gates of hell? All of these are just a few of the questions you will be able to answer after examining the scientific studies, personal testimonies, and experiences of those who say they have already traveled to heaven and back. Contemplate as we discover the astounding level to which modern science has raised the search for heaven in response to the overwhelming demand for answers.

Recent advances in medical technology have allowed doctors to bring people back from the brink of death . . . or beyond death. These medical miracles have given rise to the phenomenon of the "Near-Death Experience" (NDE), where people who slip from the doctors' grasp and come back to life, bringing with them remarkably vivid visions of heaven. They tell about visions of a bright Light—or being surrounded by overwhelming love—even talking to Jesus, Himself. This book looks closely at several of the most astounding NDEs—including contemporary experiences, as well as the experiences of biblical characters, such as the Apostle Paul, Stephen the Martyr, Elijah the Prophet and others.

This book answers questions you may have about immortality. Read the testimonies of many highly respected medical doctors, physicists, biblical scholars and scientists from the late 17th Century until today, who have been working to prove that immortality is indeed a reality. Discover the results of several scientific studies, including one 25-year project, that concluded, "For the first time in 8,000 years of recorded history, it can now be said with certainty that our mind, memory, personality and soul will survive physical death."

Examine the facts. Meet the men and women who have devoted their lives to finding the answers. Read their compelling testimonies. Take a look at the evidence. Decide for yourself. Explore *The Evidence For Heaven*!

INTRODUCTION

Where did mankind come from? Why are we here? Where are we going? We believe the answers to these questions are found in the Bible. We accept those answers on faith alone. But, what about those who are not willing to begin their journey by faith or those who are looking for more substantial evidence? With that in mind, it's not surprising that modern science has elevated the search for heaven in the halls of science. Could it be that even the scientific community is responding to that insatiable need to know more about life itself and what lies beyond it? Current studies reveal that a vast majority the world over professes a belief in life after death and in a place called heaven. Many of us believe in heaven and have at least an idea of what it's like, but for all of us, there are some unanswered questions.

Our search for heaven will bring us face to face with some research experts, Bible scholars, and scientists active in searching for the evidence that will provide critical answers—perhaps answers to your own questions or those that others have asked you. Certainly, most tend to believe that our destiny is heaven. But what are the biblical signposts that will guide us on the path of discovery? Are there spiritual truths that can be tested objectively? If we find the borders of heaven, will be also discover the gates of hell?

David W. Balsiger
Charles E. Sellier

PART 1

LIFE BEYOND

Life Beyond 1

"Rejoice and be exceeding glad, for great is your reward in heaven" (Matthew 5:12).

In the beginning God created the heavens and the earth. These first words of the Bible establish God as the eternal creator of all things, including heaven and earth. From that beginning, right through to Revelation, there are many references to heaven. Deuteronomy tells us heaven—even the highest heaven—belongs to God,[1] and that it was from heaven that God's voice was heard at the Baptism of Jesus.[2] Elijah went up in a whirlwind to the third heaven,[3] and Isaiah implores us to "lift your eyes and look to the heavens."[4] Paul tells us that he was caught up to heaven.[5] The book of Revelation tells us that there will be a new heaven, a new earth and the dwelling of God will be with men.[6]

These and dozens of other Scriptural references give us assurance that heaven is a real place. Dr. Tim Sheets, author of *Heaven Made Real*,[7] says, "The book of Hebrews, chapters 8 and 9, teaches that heaven is more real than earth itself. It's important that we understand the realness of heaven and set our eyes on a real place where we are really going to spend eternity."[8]

Heaven is a spiritual realm and believing in its existence requires faith. We're told in the Bible that without faith we can't please God, because we must come to Him by faith. Could it be that finally after 6,000 years, evidence is emerging that could prove that heaven exists? Mighty cathedrals with lofty spires and humble village chapels have all been built with the hope of heaven as part of the architects' plan, but from the most humble brick layer to the most powerful king, this magnificent outpouring has its foundation in faith. Could it be that we're at the beginning of a whole new era of knowledge and understanding? Is evidence compelling enough now to convince the skeptics, even scientists?

With recent advances in medical science and technology, more and more people are coming back from the brink of death. These medical miracles have given rise to recognizing a phenomenon known as "Near-Death Experience." When a person slips from life's grasp and appears to "die," but comes back to life, then he or she is said to have had a "Near-Death Experience, or "NDE." These people bring back with them remarkably vivid visions that frankly defy explanation, visions that are entirely consistent with all the beliefs normally associated with heaven.

It is from Near-Death Experiences that we catch a credible glimpse of heaven.

Dr. Kenneth Ring, Professor Emeritus of Psychology at the University of Connecticut and author of *Lessons from the Light*, has worked with a number of these people. He reports that, "In many of these Near-Death Experiences, people talk about a feeling of tremendous peace and wellbeing. They often say that they find themselves out of their physical body and are able to see it as though a spectator from an elevated position. Many people experience traveling through a dark space, sometimes being described like a tunnel. Then they find themselves in the presence of a radiating light of astonishing beauty and a feeling of love and great tenderness comes over them. Some people also talk about having a life review, in which they see virtually everything that's happened in their life up to that point. Many say at this time, they either made the decision they had to go back to their bodies or were told they had to go back, that their work here was not finished. These are some, but not all inclusive of typical features of a Near-Death Experience."[9]

There are definite other aspects of the Near-Death Experience that appear to go beyond the memory of the actual event, and center on the immediate things going on around the person who has just "died"— things witnessed and verified by other people who are present at the scene of death. Commonly a person will be able to recount conversations that took place in the room or remember people who came and went.

END NOTES

1. "Indeed heaven and the highest heavens belong to the LORD your God, also the earth with all that is in it" (Deuteronomy 10:14-15 NKJV).

2. "When He had been baptized, Jesus came up immediately from the water; and behold, the heavens were opened to Him, and He saw the Spirit of God descending like a dove and alighting upon Him. And suddenly a voice came from heaven, saying, 'This is My beloved Son, in whom I am well pleased'" (Matthew 3:16-17 NKJV).

3. "And it came to pass, as they still went on, and talked, that, behold, there appeared a chariot of fire, and horses of fire, and parted them both asunder; and Elijah went up by a whirlwind into heaven" (2 Kings 2:11).

4. "Lift up your eyes to the heavens, and look upon the earth beneath: for the heavens shall vanish away like smoke, and the earth shall wax old like a garment, and they that dwell therein shall die in like manner: but my salvation shall be for ever, and my righteousness shall not be abolished" (Isaiah 51:6).

5. "I knew a man in Christ above fourteen years ago, (whether in the body, I cannot tell; or whether out of the body, I cannot tell: God knoweth;) such an one caught up to the third heaven" (2 Corinthians 12:2).

6. "And I saw a new heaven and a new earth: for the first heaven and the first earth were passed away; and there was no more sea" (Revelation 21:1).

7. From an interview by Dr. Tim Sheets, *The Evidence for Heaven* by Producer David W. Balsiger, Supervising Producer Charles, E. Sellier, and Executive Producers Don and Carol Scifres, Grizzly Adams Productions, Inc., Baker, Oregon, 2004
Sheets is the author of **Heaven Made Real,** Destiny Image Publishers, Shippensburg, Pennsylvania, 1996.

8. Hebrews 8
[1]Now of the things which we have spoken this is the sum: We have such an high priest, who is set on the right hand of the throne of the Majesty in the heavens; [2]A minister of the sanctuary, and of the true tabernacle, which the Lord pitched, and not man. [3]For every high priest is ordained to offer gifts and sacrifices: wherefore it is of necessity that this man have somewhat also to offer. [4]For if he were on earth, he should not be a priest, seeing that there are priests that offer gifts according to

the law: [5]Who serve unto the example and shadow of heavenly things, as Moses was admonished of God when he was about to make the tabernacle: for, See, saith he, that thou make all things according to the pattern shewed to thee in the mount. [6]But now hath he obtained a more excellent ministry, by how much also he is the mediator of a better covenant, which was established upon better promises. [7]For if that first covenant had been faultless, then should no place have been sought for the second. [8]For finding fault with them, he saith, Behold, the days come, saith the Lord, when I will make a new covenant with the house of Israel and with the house of Judah: [9]Not according to the covenant that I made with their fathers in the day when I took them by the hand to lead them out of the land of Egypt; because they continued not in my covenant, and I regarded them not, saith the Lord. [10]For this is the covenant that I will make with the house of Israel after those days, saith the Lord; I will put my laws into their mind, and write them in their hearts: and I will be to them a God, and they shall be to me a people: [11]And they shall not teach every man his neighbour, and every man his brother, saying, Know the Lord: for all shall know me, from the least to the greatest. [12]For I will be merciful to their unrighteousness, and their sins and their iniquities will I remember no more. [13]In that he saith, A new covenant, he hath made the first old. Now that which decayeth and waxeth old is ready to vanish away.

Hebrews 9

[1]Then verily the first covenant had also ordinances of divine service, and a worldly sanctuary. [2]For there was a tabernacle made; the first, wherein was the candlestick, and the table, and the shewbread; which is called the sanctuary. [3]And after the second veil, the tabernacle which is called the Holiest of all; [4]had the golden censer, and the ark of the covenant overlaid round about with gold, wherein was the golden pot that had manna, and Aaron's rod that budded, and the tables of the covenant; [5]And over it the cherubims of glory shadowing the mercyseat; of which we cannot now speak particularly. [6]Now when these things were thus ordained, the priests went always into the first tabernacle, accomplishing the service of God. [7]But into the second went the high priest alone once every year, not without blood, which he offered for himself, and for the errors of the people: [8]The Holy Ghost this signifying, that the way into the holiest of all was not yet made manifest, while as the first tabernacle was yet standing: [9]Which was a figure for the time then present, in which were offered both gifts and sacrifices, that could not make him that did the service perfect, as pertaining to the conscience; [10]Which stood only in meats and drinks, and divers washings, and carnal ordinances, imposed on them until the time of reformation. [11]But Christ being come an high priest of good things to come, by a greater and more perfect

tabernacle, not made with hands, that is to say, not of this building; [12]Neither by the blood of goats and calves, but by his own blood he entered in once into the holy place, having obtained eternal redemption for us. [13]For if the blood of bulls and of goats, and the ashes of an heifer sprinkling the unclean, sanctifieth to the purifying of the flesh: [14]How much more shall the blood of Christ, who through the eternal Spirit offered himself without spot to God, purge your conscience from dead works to serve the living God? [15]And for this cause he is the mediator of the new testament, that by means of death, for the redemption of the transgressions that were under the first testament, they which are called might receive the promise of eternal inheritance. [16]For where a testament is, there must also of necessity be the death of the testator. [17]For a testament is of force after men are dead: otherwise it is of no strength at all while the testator liveth. [18]Whereupon neither the first testament was dedicated without blood [19]For when Moses had spoken every precept to all the people according to the law, he took the blood of calves and of goats, with water, and scarlet wool, and hyssop, and sprinkled both the book, and all the people, [20]Saying, This is the blood of the testament which God hath enjoined unto you. [21]Moreover he sprinkled with blood both the tabernacle, and all the vessels of the ministry. [22]And almost all things are by the law purged with blood; and without shedding of blood is no remission. [23]It was therefore necessary that the patterns of things in the heavens should be purified with these; but the heavenly things themselves with better sacrifices than these. [24]For Christ is not entered into the holy places made with hands, which are the figures of the true; but into heaven itself, now to appear in the presence of God for us: [25]Nor yet that he should offer himself often, as the high priest entereth into the holy place every year with blood of others; [26]For then must he often have suffered since the foundation of the world: but now once in the end of the world hath he appeared to put away sin by the sacrifice of himself. [27]And as it is appointed unto men once to die, but after this the judgment: [28]So Christ was once offered to bear the sins of many; and unto them that look for him shall he appear the second time without sin unto salvation.

9. From an interview by Kenneth Ring, Ph.D, *The Evidence for Heaven* by Producer David W. Balsiger, Supervising Producer Charles, E. Sellier, and Executive Producers Don and Carol Scifres, Grizzly Adams Productions, Inc., Baker, Oregon, 2004.
Dr. Ring is author of *Lessons From the Light – What We Can Learn from the Near-Death Experience,* Moment Point Press, Portsmouth, New Hampshire, 1998. Dr. Ring is Professor Emeritus of Psychology at the University of Connecticut and co-founder and past president

of the International Association for Near-Death Studies.

Glimpses into the Moments After Death 2

"From that time Jesus began to preach, and to say, Repent: for the kingdom of heaven is at hand" (Matthew 4:17 NKJV).

Let's meet some articulate people who have crossed from life into death, returning with amazing stories of journeys that have much to teach us.

The Red Shoe

The emergency room staff at Hartford Hospital worked feverishly to revive the young woman who had quietly slipped away from them in a sigh. Trauma team members are warriors who battle against death, and the physician on duty that afternoon was no exception. He quietly barked orders across the bed at his nurse, who knew the drill well. Without taking her eyes off the doctor's face nor having to look where she reached, she pulled up two defibrillator paddles and gelled them in one swift move. She rubbed them together and thrust them toward the doctor. His reach met hers over the bed in a precise choreography they had practiced many times. He gripped the paddles in his skilled hands, and, reaching through the tangle of monitor leads, IV lines, and oxygen tubing, applied them to the patient's chest as the nurse turned and set the defibrillator to the correct charge.

"Clear!" he ordered. The nurse stood back. The doctor fired the defibrillator. Both looked anxiously at the heart rate monitor displaying only a flat line. "Again!" he ordered, "Clear!" He fired again ... but nothing.

They gazed at each other with a look of resignation that comes from years of experience. The doctor took the young woman's chart, noted time of death, and taking a deep breath, prepared to face her family. In spite of heroic efforts, even the best physicians are sometimes forced to just "give up." Amazingly, in this particular instance, the patient did not. According to all medical and physical science, what happened in this emergency room was ... well ... impossible.

The young woman opened her eyes and drew a ragged breath. Both the physician and nurse were startled, knowing only moments before they had watched all the monitoring equipment confirm that she was dead. She murmured and struggled against the oxygen mask that had been turned off. At first, the physician and nurse thought she was only trying to breathe, but no. She was trying to talk, trying to tell them something ... something exciting.

The physician lifted the mask so that he could hear her. The young woman excitedly whispered, "I saw the most amazing thing." The woman told them that she had left her body entirely while those in the room had been working to revive her. She felt herself being pulled up through several floors of the hospital until she found herself on the roof. While looking around, enjoying the view of the skyline, she noticed something red out of the corner of her eye. It was, she said, a shoe ... a lone red shoe. Obviously everyone was extremely skeptical. After all, hadn't she just been completely comatose? Wasn't this story of being pulled up through the floors of the hospital to the roof the rambling of a woman who had just had a dream? How probable was it that a single red shoe would be on the roof of a towering, multi-story medical facility? The medical staff listened politely, but the woman would not be dissuaded.[1]

When Raymond Moody, MD, and author of *Life After Life*, heard about it, he was much more inclined to accept the woman's story, as he has researched hundreds of these kinds of events.

Dr. Moody confirms, "The Near-Death Experience is a powerful statement of the reality of the afterlife. As resuscitation techniques improve, more and more people are having profoundly meaningful experiences when they return from the verge of death. They tell us that they find themselves out of their bodies and yet still functioning and alive. As a medical doctor, I began my clinical investigations of these experiences somewhat dubious and then quickly realized that we can only ignore the evidence so long.

"Eventually, the reality of what's happening sets in and you become aware that the only way of accounting for the decisive commonalities of these experiences is to assume their validity."[2]

At Hartford Hospital, inevitably and eventually someone decided to check out the woman's story, perhaps only to put it to rest as fantasy. It was simple enough to just send someone to the roof in search of the red shoe, so an orderly was dispatched to carry out the task. Soberly returning a few minutes later with the red shoe, he simply pressed it into the doctor's hand ... and silently walked away.

Under any circumstance, it seems highly unlikely that a woman brought into the emergency room in a coma could have any knowledge of a red shoe on the roof of the hospital. But it takes more than anecdotal evidence, even as compelling as this, to achieve scientific credibility.

What was needed was a specific scientific way to demonstrate that the body and the spirit could exist separately. Such a discovery would provide strong evidence for life after death. But how could this be? Sometimes answers come from the least expected sources.

Pam Reynolds

In this case, the unlikely source was a woman named Pam Reynolds. A stunning array of medical instruments, which later provided scientific measurements were in place at the very moment of Pam Reynolds' death, which makes her story of Near-Death Experience astonishing not only in content, but also in credibility.

At age 35, Pam was diagnosed with a life-threatening brain aneurysm. An aneurysm is a weakness in the wall of an artery, very much like a large bubble in the wall of a rubber inner tube. It's a point of weakness, so under pressure, it bulges. Given the right circumstances it will rupture. In an inner tube, the tire goes flat. In a brain aneurysm, blood drains rapidly through the leak, placing the person at serious risk of immediate death. Such was the case with Pam.

The doctors located an aneurysm the size of a baseball at the base of her brain. They determined it must be removed before it ruptured and killed her. Her only hope was a boldly radical, very unusual operation. In order to fix the problem and save her life, the doctors would have to drain the blood out of her head. What's more, her body temperature would have to be lowered to 60 degrees, and her breathing would be stopped completely. She would be put into full cardiac arrest, resulting in her brain waves being flattened. Doctors who perform this dangerous procedure call it "Standstill," because for all intents and purposes, the patient is clinically dead.

In the case of Pam Reynolds, one of the surgeons' main concerns was seizure activity, which could prove deadly during such a delicate procedure. To guard against this and other complications, Pam's brain and body were extensively monitored with highly technical instruments, circumstances that make what happened next even more intriguing.

Pam's blood was drained through hoses and circulated through a bypass machine that chilled it before it was returned to her body.

It took only 10 minutes for her core body temperature to drop 25 degrees. Her heart started to flutter and falter, indicating that it would soon cease to function. The physicians triggered full cardiac arrest with a massive bolus of potassium chloride. As Pam's heart stopped, her brain waves flattened, and her brain-stem function deteriorated. Within 20 minutes, her core body temperature fell to 60 degrees, causing Pam's brain to completely shut down. Pam Reynolds now lay clinically dead. At that moment, the head of the operating table was tipped up and the bypass machine was turned off. Her physician describes it as, "the blood drained from Pam's body like oil from a car."

The surgeons began their work and Pam began an odyssey even more amazing than this daring surgery.

Pam later told the doctors she first heard a sound, likening it to a natural D on the musical scale. The sound felt like it was drawing her through the top of her head. She left her body and became a spectator to what they were doing, but noted later that her vision "was not like normal vision. It was brighter, more focused and clearer than normal vision." She stated it was like, "being pulled, but not against your will. I was going on my own accord because I wanted to go." Later she was able to describe people, procedures and even medical instruments she could not possibly have seen. She remarked that she thought the way they had shaved her head was "peculiar."[3]

Dr. Michael Sabom, cardiologist and the author of *Light and Death*, verifies, "Pam Reynolds had a very deep Near-Death Experience. At the time she had no documented brainwave activity nor brain stem activity. Actually the blood had been physically drained from her head. So, this eliminates the possibility that this was a seizure phenomenon, because during her experience, she had no seizure activity on the EEG. In addition, she had plugs in both of her ears, so she could not have heard what was discussed in the operating room during the surgical procedure. Yet, she was able to accurately recall discussions going on among the surgeons at the time that she was having her experience."[4]

Remember that every bodily reflex was being monitored, and she was in a profoundly inactive state. Despite this, Pam Reynolds was able somehow to describe a particular surgical instrument in amazing detail, a tool she would later say looked like an "electrical toothbrush with a dent in it." She even noticed that the tool had interchangeable blades kept in something that looked like a socket wrench case. Unknowingly, Pam accurately described the instrument, its attachments, the case, and even the sound it made when the surgeon used it.

Even more incredible is that Pam experienced a tunnel vortex and could hear her grandmother calling her. She continued down the dark shaft toward a pinpoint of light that kept growing larger until it was bright. She saw figures in the light, describing them as the source of light itself. She recognized many of them. They took care of her, but would not allow her to go beyond a specific point. She then knew she had to go back.

As the surgeons drained the blood from Pam's brain, the aneurysm deflated and was surgically removed. Repair to the artery was completed, and the surgeons closed the incision. The bypass machine again circulated warm blood back into her body, and very slowly brain wave patterns began to register on the monitors. Pam's body was returning to life when her heart began to exhibit erratic rhythms. Her physicians applied the defibrillation paddles and shocked her heart back into normal rhythm.

While surgeons battled to save her life, Pam was in a battle of her own. She had a dilemma. She wanted to stay with her grandmother and loved ones in that heavenly realm, but clearly understood that she was meant to return to her body. Her uncle accompanied her back up through the tunnel and instructed her to "jump," as one would into a swimming pool. She was unwilling, but her body was pulling and the tunnel was pushing, so she made the painful leap back into icy flesh and bone. When she regained consciousness, the surgery had been successfully completed, she had been revived and was now on a ventilator.

The story of the tunnel and her loved ones was certainly interesting and entirely consistent with other accounts of Near-Death Experiences, but what caught Dr. Sabom's attention were the aspects of her report that were not only accurate, but verifiable, by her surgeon and other medical professionals who were present in the operating room. During the operation, Pam's ears had been deliberately plugged by the surgical team. How could she hear conversation? How could she correctly identify the specific song—*Hotel California*—they were playing in the operating room as she reentered her body? How could she describe with such amazing accuracy the details of what took place in the operating room when, according to the many monitoring devices and verified by the surgeons, the profusionist, and the anesthesiologist, she was indeed clinically dead? Being as fully monitored as a patient can be left no room to doubt the findings.

Pam Reynolds' case was so thoroughly unique and unexplainable that Dr. Sabom conducted an extensive inquiry into and evaluation of her experience. He says, "The process of death is now understood to be a process, and not a point in time. It starts with normal waking reality and ends up in irreversible death. During this process the body dies at different rates. The problem we have as scientists and physicians is to determine when the brain is actually dead— when the person is actually dead."

Being close to death, or even at the brink, is not the same as being dead.

Dr. J.P. Moreland, Professor of Philosophy at Biola University and author of *Immortality: The Other Side of Death*, finds this kind of experience compelling. He says, "The most provocative evidence for heaven from Near-Death Experiences seems to me to be cases where people come back having information there's no way they could have had if they'd had only physical experiences while on an operating table.

"For example, some people come back, and they're able to recount conversations that their relatives have had five blocks from the hospital. On other occasions, people have actually had experiences of objects on the hospital roof, or somewhere else. When someone goes to investigate whether or not the experiences were real, they see the objects just as the people described them.

"On other occasions, people have met dead relatives who have died just about the time they had the Near-Death Experience. They've come back and reported the death of a relative that no one in the operating room knew about. This provides strong proof that there's more going on than just the lack of oxygen to the brain."[5]

Thetus Tenney

Some NDEs leave the person in a profound state of euphoria, even in the face of tragedy. Meet Thetus Tenney, International Coordinator for World Network of Prayer.

She says, "I've had a very personal experience: an automobile accident in 1975. My spirit left my body in the emergency room. It was a very real thing. I saw the doctors. I saw my body. And yet, I was enjoying a tremendous peace, even as I watched my body in pain. It was just a glorious experience. It was just as real as physical life, but there was a spiritual atmosphere to the whole thing, so I do believe in life after death. I know it exists. I have experienced it."

All of these people appear to have discovered something beyond the experience of the rest of us. Will we have to die to find out, or is there perhaps something to be gained from their depth of knowledge? Someone once said, "The wise learn from experience; the wisest learn from the experience of others."

Thetus Tenney adds, "When my spirit left my body, during the time I was experiencing this wonderful peace, I became concerned about my friend being worried. And when I thought about him at church, it was as though my spirit was transported there. I saw my friend, who was the guest speaker that morning. I saw him go to the piano, saw him read his Scripture text. I even saw the Bible.

"Later that evening, my sister was in the room with me. I had a private room. She was telling me about what comfort they had at the church service that morning. It was annoying me because I wasn't feeling well, and I wanted her to quit talking, so I told her, 'Yes, I know all about it,' and finished her sentences, telling her what had happened at church. She knew my body was in an emergency room while this was taking place, but my spirit was in church.

"A few days later, my friend who had been the guest minister that morning, heard about my experience and came to see me. He had heard that I had seen him in the pulpit. I told him, 'Cleveland, I saw the page from which you read.' And I described it—that his text had been marked with red. So he brought his Bible over and opened it up, and it was exactly the way I described it, as though I had been looking over his shoulder when he read the text to the congregation that morning."[6]

These experiences would seem to lend one more bit of evidence that the spirit continues to live on after the body dies. But lives on where? Where does that spirit go? Are we any closer to identifying the place those spirits might reside? Perhaps we're getting closer to discovering the reality of heaven.

END NOTES

1. Story reenacted in *The Evidence for Heaven* by Producer David W. Balsiger, Supervising Producer Charles, E. Sellier, and Executive Producers Don and Carol Scifres, Grizzly Adams Productions, Inc., Baker, Oregon, 2004.

2. From an interview with Raymond Moody, M.D., *The Evidence for Heaven* by Producer David W. Balsiger, Supervising Producer Charles, E. Sellier, and Executive Producers Don and Carol Scifres, Grizzly Adams Productions, Inc., Baker, Oregon, 2004. Dr. Moody is the author of *Life After Life – The Investigation of a Phenomenon – Survival of Bodily Death,* Harper San Francisco (Harper Collins Publishers), 2000.

3. Story reenacted in *The Evidence for Heaven* by Producer David W. Balsiger, Supervising Producer Charles, E. Sellier, and Executive Producers Don and Carol Scifres, Grizzly Adams Productions, Inc., Baker, Oregon, 2004.

4. From an interview with Michael Sabom, M.D., *The Evidence for Heaven* by Producer David W. Balsiger, Supervising Producer Charles, E. Sellier, and Executive Producers Don and Carol Scifres, Grizzly Adams Productions, Inc., Baker, Oregon, 2004. Dr.

Sabom is the author of *Light & Death – One Doctor's Fascinating Account of Near-Death Experiences,* Zondervan Publishing House, Grand Rapids, Michigan, 1998.

5. From an interview with Dr. J.P. Moreland, *The Evidence for Heaven* by Producer David W. Balsiger, Supervising Producer Charles, E. Sellier, and Executive Producers Don and Carol Scifres, Grizzly Adams Productions, Inc., Baker, Oregon, 2004. Dr. Moreland is a Professor of Philosophy at Bible University and one of the authors of *Immortality: The Other Side of Death*, Thomas Nelson, 1992. Moreland is The Distinguished Professor of Philosophy at Talbot School of Theology, Biola University, in La Mirada, California.

6. From an interview with Thetus Tenney, *The Evidence for Heaven* by Producer David W. Balsiger, Supervising Producer Charles, E. Sellier, and Executive Producers Don and Carol Scifres, Grizzly Adams Productions, Inc., Baker, Oregon, 2004. Ms. Tenney is with the God Chaser's Network in Pineville, Louisiana, and serves as the International Coordinator of the World Network of Prayer. She has authored *Prayer Takes Wings*.

The Near-Death Experience 3

"But lay up your treasures in heaven ..."
(Matthew 6:2 (NKJV).

𝔉aith is sufficient for most Christians when considering the reality of heaven, but for some, it would be reassuring if some cold, hard facts could back up the Scriptural descriptions and promises. The good news is that science is catching up. New clues in the search for and evidence supporting the reality of heaven are being uncovered even in the halls of science.

"The most provocative evidence that comes from NDEs is the fact that when you're having these experiences, you're doing things you can't do in your normal, everyday, waking, bodily life. For example, you can fly. Or you can travel instantly from one place to another place," says Dr. Fred Wolf, author of *The Spiritual Universe*. "To me, this is indicative of the heavenly realm. The major problem with the medical profession, and in fact, science in general today, is that they refute completely anything that is outside the materialist realm. Therefore, if a person were to have an unusual experience such as an out-of-body experience or an NDE, or for that matter, even appear at the Pearly Gates themselves, no doctor would be able to deal with this experience, because, by definition, such an experience cannot take place."[1]

Is there any way to reconcile the scientific and anecdotal evidence? In order for a concept to be judged "scientific," certain specific rules must apply. For example, for a theory to be regarded as scientifically credible, it must rest on a firm foundation of knowledge derived from facts and principles determined through scientific disciplines and protocols. The question then is, "Does the anecdotal evidence of NDEs, established by medical experts, lend itself to scientific scrutiny?"

Raymond Moody, MD, PhD, author of *Life After Life*, has developed a large body of work that suggests that indeed it does. He says, "I began my research by talking with about 150 people who had been to the brink of death and had experiences. I was able to identify 15 common elements that occur in these experiences, regardless of the sex, age or medical condition of the patient.

"In many instances, when a person reaches the point of greatest physical distress, they often hear themselves pronounced "dead" by the attending physician. They hear an uncomfortable noise and feel themselves moving very rapidly through some sort of aperture like a tunnel. They find themselves outside their bodies, watching the resuscitation attempts as a spectator. Soon a variety of things begins to happen, such as others from the beyond come to meet them. Glimpsing the spirits of relatives and friends who have already passed away is common. And they find themselves welcomed by a love that's beyond anything they've ever known.

"With regularity, it is recounted that at some point, a being of light and love appears, asking them questions, while enabling them to review a panorama consisting of every event of their lives. At some critical juncture, they are told that they must go back to earth."[2]

With uncanny regularity, fifteen separate elements seem to be commonly remembered by those who encounter an NDE, although some may not experience all fifteen elements.

(1) **There are not words to describe it.** Many of those who have experienced an NDE say that no words can adequately or truly describe what happened to them. The experience, for them, is inexpressible. Although they can report certain events, the overall impression is beyond their ability to describe it.

(2) **They heard themselves pronounced dead.** Many of them relate hearing a medical person pronounce them dead. To those around them, all their bodily signs indicated that they had expired, but during that moment, they perceived they were "still alive."

(3) **They felt peaceful.** Many people recall feeling sensations of extreme pleasure.

Although severe pain normally accompanies a life-threatening injury or disease, only feelings of deep peace and quietude during the NDE are what is recalled.

(4) They heard a noise. Many relate hearing a distinct sound that occurs either at or near death. In some cases, this noise can be quite pleasant, like rapturous music. In other cases, the noise can be harsh and disturbing, marked by a continuous tone, buzzing or banging.

(5) They traveled down a dark tunnel toward a bright light. Many describe being propelled or drawn through some dark passageway, while hearing an accompanying noise such as previously described. This dark passageway has been variously described as a tunnel, shaft, cave, sewer, trough, valley, and so on.

(6) They were outside their bodies, observing. Remembrance of seeing their physical bodies apart from themselves, as though they were "spectators" observing, is very commonly retold. Surprise, panic, and a desire to return to their bodies sometimes accompanied the realization that they were separate from their physical form. Others seemed to be emotionally detached, merely observing with interest.

(7) **Others arrived to meet them.** In many cases they encountered spiritual entities, who were present to help them through the experience. These beings variously appeared as loved ones who had recently passed away, strangers who had died, or other spirits who were acting as their guardians. Even if the spirit was unknown to the person, there seemed to have been no fear experienced on their behalf.

(8) **They were in the presence of a Being of Light.** Quite a few speak of beholding a brilliant light that, despite its brilliance, did not hurt their eyes or cause them to shy from it. The consensus has been that this radiance is far more than just a mere light, but a supernatural being or a heavenly personality. Rather than fear, they were filled with an overwhelming desire to be in the presence of this being, who only emanated love, warmth and peace. One whose communication with them was of a telepathic nature—through

conveyed thoughts void of audible tones—involving aspects of, or pertaining to, the purpose and meaning of their lives.

(9) **They reviewed their lives.** A number of them recall a particular moment of time during their experience in which they witnessed a vivid, panoramic review of their lives. These images, coupled with the realization of a higher power and an obvious afterlife, provoked in them the importance of loving people and living life with new meaning.

(10) **They knew they had to return.** Some describe being prevented or restricted from traveling beyond a certain point in their journey or from reaching the being of light. An array of types of barriers mentioned were persons, fences, doors, and bodies of water. In addition, others spoke of an imaginary line or invisible barrier. Some simply describe it as a "knowing" or "willful acknowledgment" of the limit through unspoken conversation with their guides. This, more commonly than not, is reported to be the moment or point at which most realize that returning to his or her physical body is now required.

(11) **They returned.** All obviously returned from their Near-Death Experience, but how each felt about coming back varies considerably. Some wanted to stay with the being of light, while others felt obliged to return in order to complete unfinished tasks. There were those who made a conscious decision to return, yet others—reluctant to leave this wonderful place—were told to go.

In any case, the return is often instantaneous—back through the dark tunnel. Commonly expressed was a feeling of being pulled or drawn by a force, back to the material world and the return into their physical body being as unpleasant as leaping into a pool of cold water.

(12) **Some tell of the experience; some do not.** Those who have had NDEs regard their experience as a real event rather than a dream. But since they believe that it was extraordinarily unique and that others would be skeptical, they are sometimes reluctant about disclosing their experiences, which they feel are inexpressible anyway.

(13) Lives change. Having a glimpse into the "beyond" and experiencing the world of the supernatural tends to change people for the better. Not only are they likely to live more deliberately (having been given a second chance), but, also, they are more caring for other people. Nearly all seem to have a better understanding of the meaning of life and a new purpose in living.

(14) Death holds no fear. Most who experience an NDE no longer fear death, now viewing death as just a transitional state to another dimension or form of life.

(15) Other people can corroborate the NDE experience. Sometimes there are independent testimonies of people who have corroborated some of the details in NDE accounts. For example, a patient who "dies" on the operating table might describe events and conversations that the surgeons can verify.

Other researchers have identified some additional commonalities:

Mental telepathy – Whether or not there is spoken word, there is communication, and it is very clearly understood. No one seems to question this ability, not even the newly arrived.

Clear thoughts – Some people experience mental clarity, acuity, and fluidity beyond that which they ever experienced in life. This might be especially true of people who were suffering impairment at the time of death. When the impairment is lifted with the death of the damaged human body, and the soul is pure and free again, then thought is easy.

Tremendous ecstasy – Many people report feelings of incomprehensible joy, overwhelming love and abundant peace. These feelings account for the reluctance (even if momentary) of people to desire returning to life. Even if the reasons to return are compelling, such as a young mother who knows her children need her, yet she struggles with her own will to go back.

Unlimited knowledge – There seems to be instantaneous access to information and enlightenment of the mind, which lends enormous credibility to biblical accounts of the same.

Seeing the future – Occasionally, people report that they are given a glimpse into a possible future (along the same principle of Ebenezer Scrooge when he was taken on a journey into the future with the Ghost of Christmas Future). Many return with a sense of mission or renewed purpose.

Fear – While most people describe peace, quietude (and even curiosity), some people are terrified, even if the outcome of the experience promises to be one of love, peace and joy. Not only does shock set in, but also overwhelming confusion and anxiety over unknown factors. What just happened? Am I dead? How is this possible? Help me! What's happening? Am I going to hell?

A sense of belonging or coming home – To some people, the experience seems somehow comfortingly familiar—less about death and more about homecoming. Even though they've never been dead before, there is a sense that they already know what's going on and what will happen, and they welcome it. This is more common to persons of faith and those anticipating heaven in their eternal existence and afterlife. This sense is enhanced by the arrival of familiar people such as family members and friends who have already passed over. In some cases, people actually identify Jesus Christ in the experience, so they are comforted and calm.

Not everyone experiences the NDE in quite the same way, but the commonalities are so striking, they're worth noting. But what about after the person returns to us? Are there also commonalities there, as well? Does coming face to face with the dynamic of a heavenly realm change a person forever?

How Do People Change After an NDE?
Interestingly, in almost all Near-Death Experiences, the person desires to stay, but for various reasons is required or chooses to come back. Amazingly, the majority, upon return, report a complete loss of any further fear of death. But other, more profound changes may also occur.

Melvin Morse, MD, neuroscientist, researcher, and author of *Transformed by the Light*, says, "We learned that having an NDE transforms someone for life in very healthy, nurturing, life-fulfilling ways. Specifically:

- they give more money to charity.
- they're more involved with their communities.
- they spend more time with their families.
- they volunteer more hours in terms of volunteering at the hospital or local charities.
- they're uniquely involved with living life.

"We learn that there's not only a psychological transformation, but there are physical changes that we could document, as well. These physical changes include that their watches frequently would break or not work. They demagnetize their credit cards. Their immune systems would function better. And they would often have heightened intelligence as a result of the experience," according to medical doctor Melvin Morse.[3]

Around eighty percent of the people who experienced near-death claim that their lives have been forever changed by what happened to them. Various researchers have attempted to profile these changes over the years, not just because it's interesting to note how people change, but to give comfort to a person who has experienced an NDE and is confused by the transformations. It's important for that individual to know that he is not alone and can find understanding and solace through the common bonds now shared with other NDE survivors.

Other changes that may accompany a Near-Death Experience

An encounter with the spirit world can have profound psychological and physiological effects. Clearly a person may return as a kinder, gentler man or woman. While the effects can generally be interpreted as positive, they may also be confusing for that person and those who are close to them.

• Besides losing all fear of death, the majority of persons gravitates toward an intensely spiritual side. The encounter with the Being of Light and the overwhelming sensations of love, peace and calm are compelling evidence that God exists and He loves them. If there was ever doubt, it's usually gone.

• The person may more easily engage in abstract thinking, is more thoughtful, philosophical, and contemplative. (This can lead to temporary or occasional depression).

• People who experience NDEs commonly return to be more giving personally, professionally, and charitably.

• They love more intensely and pay more attention to meaningful relationships.

• They tend to quit "sweating the small stuff," letting go of such issues as old and painful childhood problems or a failed relationship.

• They are less competitive, less concerned about being right, and more tolerant of others.

• They are mission oriented: convinced that having been spared and returned to life has some meaning and purpose to be fulfilled.

• Sensations are often heightened.

• Intuition, discernment and judgment are heightened.

• They're more joyful and relaxed.

• They are better able to "see the big picture" in situations that would have formerly caused drama.

• They are more focused and spend more time studying, exploring and living life to the fullest.

• They no longer are more mission-oriented in a calm manner.

• Many develop a sense of timelessness. They tend to behave in a manner more "present."

• Forgiveness is easier.

• They tend to be clear about the concept of immortality and the temporary nature of this body on earth ... and just about everything else.

• They are sometimes more creative and thought patterns expand. Intelligence may heighten.

• They may be sensitive to light and sound.

• Their energy may change: mentally disturbed individuals may show marked behavioral improvements; slothful people may suddenly get into action.

• Their internal sense of time may change as if they've changed time zones.

• Blood pressure may lower. (This may be a consequence of being more peaceful.)

• Metabolism might increase.

• Interactions with medications may alter.

• They may become more sensitive to allergens, or allergies may go away.

• Patterns of eating might change.

• Electrical energies change: watches stop, microphones squelch, electrical appliances quit, cell phone calls drop, hard drives erase, etc.

Experiencing those moments just beyond death brings a person face-to-face with the light and love of God and the promise of heaven. No one returns from such an encounter without a deeper faith and a greater joy and assurance.

END NOTES

1. From an interview with Dr. Fred Alan Wolf, *The Evidence for Heaven* by Producer David W. Balsiger, Supervising Producer Charles, E. Sellier, and Executive Producers Don and Carol Scifres, Grizzly Adams Productions, Inc., Baker, Oregon, 2004. Dr. Wolf is a physicist and author of *The Spiritual Universe: How Quantum Physics Proves the Existence of the Soul*, originally published by Simon and Schuster, 1996, Moment Point Press, Inc. Portsmouth, New Hampshire, 1999. His work includes bridging gaps between the science of quantum physics and shamanism, psychology, human behavior, and spirituality.

2. From an interview with Raymond Moody, M.D., *The Evidence for Heaven* by Producer David W. Balsiger, Supervising Producer Charles, E. Sellier, and Executive Producers Don and Carol Scifres, Grizzly Adams Productions, Inc., Baker, Oregon, 2004. Dr. Moody is the author of *Life After Life – The Investigation of a Phenomenon – Survival of Bodily Death,* Harper San Francisco (Harper Collins Publishers), 2000.

3. From an interview with Melvin Morse, M.D., *The Evidence for Heaven* by Producer David W. Balsiger, Supervising Producer Charles, E. Sellier, and Executive Producers Don and Carol Scifres, Grizzly Adams Productions, Inc., Baker, Oregon, 2004. Dr. Morse is the author (with Paul Perry) of *Where God Lives,* Cliff Street Books (Imprint of Harper Collins Publishers), New York City, New York, 2000; and *Closer to the Light,* Villard Books, (Division of Random House), New York City, New York, 1990.

Part 2

When a Soul Departs

What is a Soul? 4

"And fear not them which kill the body, but are not able to kill the soul; but rather fear him which is able to destroy both soul and body in hell" (Matthew 10:28 KJV).

Almost since the dawn of time, human beings have been aware that we contain an "essence" that is not of flesh and bone, and is more than personality and intellect. It's tempting to say that the soul has been difficult to define, but in fact, many societies and cultures have done it. The problem is that many of these definitions contradict, or at least collide, with each other. Some have thought that the soul is the source of all life. Others have considered it to be the enduring resonance of a person who passes over. Some have thought that soul is the highest level of human thought. Many have divided the soul into functions that describe the abstract aspects of human nature. Yet, others have claimed it to be the defining, exclusive domain of human beings, declaring it to be completely lacking in animals. Of course, there has been little definitive research, because no scientist can "see" the soul, so to attempt to quantify and study it has been impossible ... until now.

Defining Physical Death

Before we ponder the nature of the soul and what happens when we die, it is necessary to define death from a biological standpoint. The task is not as easy as one might think. At first glance death is simply "the termination of life." The heart stops beating and the person's respiration ceases. But with today's medical advances, a terminated life can sometimes be resuscitated. If the heart stops beating, it might be possible to use CPR, medications, and defibrillation technologies to restart it. If a person stops breathing, a ventilator can be administered to artificially breathe for the person. So historical, traditional definitions of death are too simplistic in light of modern medical advances.

We also understand now that dying is a process. No matter how rapid, it's a cascade of events that takes place in a sequence that systematically shuts down the body to a point where damage can't be reversed and it can no longer be revived. The precise moment of death has been defined by law and is uniformly honored within the United States: An individual who has sustained either (1) irreversible cessation of circulatory and respiratory functions, or (2) irreversible cessation of all functions of the entire brain, including death of the brain stem. At this point, death occurs ... or does it? Just because the body ceases to function, does this mean that the person is gone? Or is there some essence of life that goes on? Is this "essence" the soul?

Research on the nature of the soul, as modern scientists would recognize it, probably departed from "theory" and made its way to the lab in the 1930s with the work of Wilder Penfield, widely acknowledged as the father of neurosurgery. He mapped the brain by electrically stimulating parts of the brain during surgery. Brain surgery is sometimes done under local anesthetic, because the brain itself has no pain receptors and cannot feel pain. His patients were awake and able to respond to him. By probing certain parts of the brain, he could elicit specific responses. One of those areas of the brain he stimulated triggered the phenomenon of the Near-Death Experience. He worked for fifty years, looking for the mind and the soul. He never found either in the brain. His conclusion: " ... the brain has not explained the mind fully."

According to Dr. Melvin Morse, there is a man who has picked up where Wilder Penfield left off. His name is Dr. Art Ward, former chairman of neurosurgery at the University of Washington. He told Dr. Morse about one of his own patients who also described the sensations associated with NDE.

When Dr. Ward stimulated one part of his brain, he reported feeling as though he was leaving his body. When Dr. Ward stimulated another part, he felt like he was being drawn through a tunnel. Dr. Ward remembered Wilder Penfield's work and hypothesized, based on his own experience, that Penfield was probably probing the right lobe of the brain to replicate the NDE sensations. Intrigued, Dr. Morse, went back through Penfield's book, and found what he was looking for. Indeed, the probing had been in the right temporal lobe, right above the ear. He was exploring a part of the brain called the Sylvan Fissure. Dr. Morse now knew where the NDE takes place in the brain, but not what happens. He was certain that the anecdotal evidence—literally thousands of identical descriptions—was sufficient to conclude that something leaves the body. But what? The soul perhaps?[1]

Let us debunk a myth now. Some people claim that upon death, the body immediately weighs less, and this is proof that the soul has left the body. Dr. Gary Posner says that's not true. He says, "At the beginning of the 20th century, measurements seemed to indicate that the human body lost about an ounce of weight seemingly at about the time of death. But as our technology has increased so that our scales are able to weigh smaller and smaller increments, the so-called one-ounce has been ratcheting down less and less. So I suspect that if we ever develop a perfect scale that can measure weight in infinitesimal units, the amount of weight that's supposedly lost at death will be infinitesimal. That leads me to the conclusion that the weight loss, if indeed real, is not a soul that weighs about an ounce, but I think it's an artifact in our ability to take perfect measurements. Perhaps just the amount of air that is no longer being inhaled into the lungs may ultimately turn out to account for this so-called weight loss."[2]

Dr. R.C. Sproul, founder of Ligonier Ministries, adds, "Well, when we talk about the body from a philosophical and physics perspective, we think of that which has extension. It takes up space and it can be measured to some degree. It's physical. When we talk about the soul, we are talking about the non-extended reality, that which cannot be measured spatially. Many people want to make a distinction between the soul and the spirit, but I think from a biblical perspective, those terms are basically interchangeable. Both refer to the non-physical aspect of our lives."[3]

So, what might the soul be? Scripturally the soul is linked to intellect, or the mind. In Psalms 139:14 (NASB), the psalmist writes, "I will give thanks to You, for I am wonderfully made; Wonderful are Your works, and my soul *knows* it very well." Or in Lamentations 3:20: "My soul *remembers* them well and is bowed down within me." Scripture also suggests that the soul is also the will. In Job 6:7 (NASB), Job says, "My soul *refuses* to touch them ..." and in Job 7:15 (NASB), he continues, "...my soul *would choose* suffocation and death rather than my pains." In addition to intellect and will, the soul is also given the attributes of human emotion. Love: "Tell me, o you whom my soul *loves*" (Song of Songs 1:7 NLV). Hate: "... who are *hated* by David's soul" (2 Samuel 5:8 NLV). And joy: "Rejoice the soul of thy servant to *rejoice* ..." (Psalm 86:4 ASV). The Bible clearly indicates that the soul is the essence of the person: all that he or she thinks and feels. It is the humans' connection with God.

Body and soul are integrated during life on earth, but they are entirely separate. Hank Hanegraaff, author of *Counterfeit Revival*, says, "I think that if you look at humanity, you're looking at a soul-soma unity, a soul-body unity. So we are not complete unless we talk about both aspects of humanity: one, the soul, the incorporeal, and the non-physical aspect. The other is the body, which is the physical aspect of humanity. At death, there is a separation between the body and soul."[4]

Is it this separation that allows the soul to move toward heaven? But if our soul survives, is there any research to tell us where it will live on?

END NOTES

1. From an interview with Melvin Morse, M.D., *The Evidence for Heaven* by Producer David W. Balsiger, Supervising Producer Charles, E. Sellier, and Executive Producers Don and Carol Scifres, Grizzly Adams Productions, Inc., Baker, Oregon, 2004. Dr. Morse is the author (with Paul Perry) of *Where God Lives,* Cliff Street Books (Imprint of Harper Collins Publishers), New York City, New York, 2000; and *Closer to the Light,* Villard Books, (Division of Random House), New York City, New York, 1990.

2 From the notes of Gary Posner, M.D., interviewed for *The Evidence for Heaven* by Producer David W. Balsiger, Supervising

Producer Charles, E. Sellier, and Executive Producers Don and Carol Scifres, Grizzly Adams Productions, Inc., Baker, Oregon, 2004. Dr. Posner is a Contributing Editor to *Scientific Review of Alternative Medicine*.

3. From an interview with Dr. R.C. Sproul, *The Evidence for Heaven* by Producer David W. Balsiger, Supervising Producer Charles, E. Sellier, and Executive Producers Don and Carol Scifres, Grizzly Adams Productions, Inc., Baker, Oregon, 2004. Dr. Sproul is the founder of Ligonier Ministries in Orlando, Florida.

4. From an interview with Hank Hanegraaff, *The Evidence for Heaven* by Producer David W. Balsiger, Supervising Producer Charles, E. Sellier, and Executive Producers Don and Carol Scifres, Grizzly Adams Productions, Inc., Baker, Oregon, 2004. Hanegraaff is the author *of The Counterfeit Revival*, Word Publishing, Dallas, Texas, 1997. He has also authored *The Bible Answer Book, The Covering, Christianity in Crisis, and the Prayer of Jesus*.

God in Heaven 5

"So then after the Lord had spoken unto them, he was received up into heaven, and sat on the right hand of God"
(Mark 16:19 KJV).

The concept of a God in heaven, who is active in the affairs of humankind, has been an important part of biblical teaching for thousands of years and is powerfully portrayed in painting, literature, and song for centuries. Interestingly, although faiths differ slightly in their concepts of God and heaven, all of them focus on the ideas of peace, serenity, and some sort of justice or retribution. These concepts seem to bridge all societal norms. According to a recent Gallup Poll, over 70 percent of those polled believed in the existence of a heaven of some kind—strong evidence indeed for the power of ideas. Or could it be the idea of a powerful God?[1]

Christianity, for example, has for centuries proclaimed that Jesus Christ died on the cross, was buried, and yet emerged from the tomb alive again. This, according to the Christian view, is a matter of historical fact.

Hank Hanegraaff, author of *Counterfeit Revival*, says, "The Christian viewpoint of heaven is ultimately communicated through Jesus Christ. Jesus Christ, who was God in human flesh, demonstrated that He was God through the immutable fact of the resurrection, so His opinion is infinitely better than my opinion or anybody else's opinion, because Christ is the Creator of the Cosmos. Christ said that He was the Way, the Truth, and the Life, that only through a relationship with Him could we be united with Him throughout all eternity, so only those who put their trust in Jesus Christ ultimately are going to spend an eternity with Him."[2]

But the immediate questions at hand are, "What's the afterlife all about? And where will we be spending it?"

Keith Harris, author of *The Unveiling*, answers the questions. He says, "Many people create their own ideas of the afterlife because they do not wish to accept the biblical accounts of heaven because to do so necessitates a belief in hell. And it's easier to create something that is wonderful than something that is possibly degrading or eternally separated from God in heaven. We are eternal beings created in the image of God who is triune in being. Therefore we are triune in being, as body and soul and spirit. Upon death, the body goes back to the dust of the earth and the spirit and soul go back to God, who gave it. When God breathed into man, man became a living soul—a part of the eternity of God. Therefore, the soul of man is eternal. Many perceive that we will live eternally in the heaven where God dwells now, when in fact, we will live eternally in the heavenly city New Jerusalem on a newly purified earth. In that city, we will have perfect peace and contentment."[3]

The Bible describes heaven as a place of incomprehensible beauty and peace, but the biblical description also offers far more.

Dr. Tim Sheets, author of *Heaven Made Real*, says, "Heaven is a place where relationships are restored, relationship with

God and relationship with friends or family that have already gone on. Heaven is also a place where destiny is fulfilled. Our time on earth is short, but our time in heaven is forever, so destiny is started here; destiny is fulfilled when we get to heaven. Heaven will be much like earth if you can think of earth as it would have been when Adam saw it: no pollution. In heaven we're told there are rivers; there are lakes; there are streams; there are trees; there are animals; there are fruit trees; there are clouds. Heaven is real. We're going to have banquets there. Heaven is a very real place; it's not a figment of the imagination."[4]

Scholars share their vision of the promise of heaven

Dr. Elmer Towns, author of *Bible Answers for Almost All Your Questions*, says, "The greatest evidence of heaven to me is the Word of God. Jesus promised a heaven to us when He said, 'In My Father's house are many mansions; if it were not so, I would have told you. I go to prepare a place for you. And if I go and prepare a place for you, I will come again and receive you to myself; that where I am, there you may be also' (John 14:2-3

NKJV). The Bible teaches that the heaven is a real place for real people who will spend a real eternity there with the Lord, enjoying all the pleasures and benefits that have been promised by God Himself. Some believe we'll be like Casper the Ghost in heaven, sitting on a cloud and playing a harp, but that's not it. A Bible scholar, A.J. Ironside, said, 'Life in heaven will not be that unlike life here on earth.' By that, he meant that we'll live on an earth that will have dirt and grass and trees and other people. We'll interact with them. But most importantly, we'll have eternal life. We'll live forever."[5]

Dr. Ron Rhodes, author *Heaven, the Undiscovered Country: Exploring the Wonder of the Afterlife*, says, "One of the great things about heaven is that death will be a thing of the past. In fact, we'll have brand new, resurrected bodies that will never grow old again. No more gray hairs. No more hair falling out. No new wrinkles showing up on your face in the morning. No cholesterol build-up. No heart problems. No fear of death whatsoever. That's one of the great things about heaven. Not only that, but we're going to have a reunion with our Christian loved ones. You know, all of us have lost someone close to us, whether it's a child or a mom or a dad. We'll be together with them again, and never will death separate us again. Scripture also indicates that in heaven, all of our needs will be met. God has promised to satisfy all of our hunger and all of our thirst. And so that's one thing that separates the heavenly sphere from the earthly sphere. Never again will we go hungry."[6]

END NOTES

1. From an interview with Hank Hanegraaff, *The Evidence for Heaven* by Producer David W. Balsiger, Supervising Producer Charles, E. Sellier, and Executive Producers Don and Carol Scifres, Grizzly Adams Productions, Inc., Baker, Oregon, 2004. Hanegraaff is the author *of The Counterfeit Revival*, Word Publishing, Dallas, Texas, 1997. He has also authored *The Bible Answer Book, The Covering, Christianity in Crisis, and the Prayer of Jesus.*

2. Ibid.

3. From an interview with Keith Harris, *The Evidence for Heaven* by Producer David W. Balsiger, Supervising Producer Charles, E. Sellier, and Executive Producers Don and Carol Scifres, Grizzly Adams Productions, Inc., Baker, Oregon, 2004. Harris has authored *The Unveiling: A Journey Through the Book of Revelation*.

4. From an interview by Dr. Tim Sheets, *The Evidence for Heaven* by Producer David W. Balsiger, Supervising Producer Charles, E. Sellier, and Executive Producers Don and Carol Scifres, Grizzly Adams Productions, Inc., Baker, Oregon, 2004. Sheets is the author of *Heaven Made Real,* Destiny Image Publishers, Shippensburg, Pennsylvania, 1996.

5. From an interview by Dr. Elmer Towns, *The Evidence for Heaven* by Producer David W. Balsiger, Supervising Producer Charles, E. Sellier, and Executive Producers Don and Carol Scifres, Grizzly Adams Productions, Inc., Baker, Oregon, 2004. Towns is the author of *Bible Answers to Almost All Your Questions*. Dr. Towns is the author of over 80 books and is the Dean of Liberty University's School of Religion.

6. From an interview by Ron Rhodes, *The Evidence for Heaven* by Producer David W. Balsiger, Supervising Producer Charles, E. Sellier, and Executive Producers Don and Carol

Scifres, Grizzly Adams Productions, Inc.,
Baker, Oregon, 2004. Rhodes is the author of
***Heaven - The Undiscovered Country:
Exploring the Wonder of the Afterlife,*** Harvest
House Publishers, Eugene, Oregon, 1996.

Where is Heaven?

"And as ye go, preach, saying, The Kingdom of heaven is at hand" (Matthew 10:7 KJV)

ℬecause we have determined that God is omnipresent—everywhere all the time, it might be problematic to attempt to "locate" Him in heaven. In a quest to discover exactly where heaven is, the believer must turn to the Bible, which serves as a very clear road atlas. We can trust the directions because, "All Scripture is given by inspiration of God, and is profitable for doctrine, for reproof, for correction, for instruction in righteousness, that the man of God may be perfect—thoroughly furnished unto all good works" (2 Timothy 3:16-17 KJV). The Bible, although written by men, is the inspired Word of God, and we can trust the truths that lie within its pages.

The Bible tells us that heaven is above us. But, it's not a fixed point in the sky like a star that can be seen only by some people at certain times when the earth's rotation and axis align perfectly in the night. It makes no difference where you stand on the globe: heaven is above you at all times. God is above you.

In Genesis 17, it says that God went *up* from Abraham.[1] In John 3 we are told that the Son of Man came *down* from heaven.[2] In Acts 1, we find that Christ went *up* into heaven [not down], and a cloud received him out of sight.[3] Job says, "Let not God regard it *from above*."[4] In Deuteronomy, we read, "who shall go *up* for us to heaven?"[5] Throughout Scripture, we are given the location of heaven as upward and beyond the firmament—the star-shimmering universe over our heads and all around us, beyond as far as the eye can see or the mind can comprehend.

Even without Scriptural confirmation, we humans "know" on some deep, spiritual level that heaven is above us. When we pray, we bow our heads down in reverent submission and respect for One above us. When we look to God, we look up. When we worship, we raise our hands. Every human gesture of joy is expressed upward. Every expression of sorrow is expressed down. Heaven is up.

Dr. R.C. Sproul, founder of Ligonier Ministries, thinks he may have an answer. "When we talk about the "where-ness" of heaven, I believe it's a place, but it's a different kind of place. It crosses a dimensional barrier. With our human concept of dimensional space, it could be right here or right next door, but in another realm transcendentally beyond the three-dimensional type of reality we experience normally."[6]

Dr. Tim Sheets, author of *Heaven Made Real*, says, "The Bible teaches that heaven is in the northernmost part of the universe. Isaiah talks about Lucifer leading a rebellion against God in the sides of the north. Job 26 talks about God making heaven and stretching it over an empty place. Scientists know there's a hole in the northernmost part of the universe. Perhaps heaven is just beyond that—about twenty-one light years away."[7]

Michael Sabom, MD, author of *Light and Death*, adds, "I think the message of the Near-Death Experience is that there is something there other than our physical reality. There is a spiritual realm. I also think there is the message that God is there. It's similar to Paul's revelation in the first chapter of Romans in the New Testament: that the Law of God is written on the hearts of all men. I think that the Near-Death Experience is bringing that to the person's awareness during the process of dying."[8]

Ralph Muncaster, author of *Going to Heaven*, says, "Some people have come to me with a question: 'Isn't there some middle ground between skeptics and believers in certain religions about this issue of heaven ... or hell, for that matter? My point of view is that there is no middle ground. Either heaven exists or it doesn't exist. The important thing is to find out, if it does exist, what is necessary, what's involved, and what authority do you use to know that it exists. When you go to the Bible and you look at the 668 historical prophesies, all shown to be true, that gives you some confidence that any future activies such as life after death and heaven, would also be true."[9]

Among a growing group of scientists who seem to be accepting of the notion of an eternal spirit is physicist Dr. Stephen W. Hawking, widely regarded to be the most brilliant scientific mind of this—or perhaps any—age. In what many regard as a complete turn-about, Dr. Hawking, in his book *The Theory of Everything: The Origin and Fate of the Universe*, writes, "It would be very difficult to explain why the universe should have begun in just this way, except as the act of a God who intended to create beings like us ... the whole history of the universe can be said to be the work of God. However, if we do discover a complete theory, it should, in time, be understandable by everyone, not just a few scientists. If we find the answer to that, it would be the ultimate triumph of human reason. For then we would know the mind of God."[10]

At long last, the discussion is out on the scientific table. And Hawking is not the only scientist who has opened his mind to the intriguing possibilities of a world that was created especially for immortal life. Nobel Prize winning biochemist, Francis Crick, states, "The origin of life appears to be almost a miracle, so many are the conditions that would have to be satisfied to get it going."[11]

The internationally renowned physicist, Paul Davis, concedes, "It is in the fundamental constants of nature that we find the most surprising evidence for a grand design."[12]

Another Nobel Prize winner in the field of physiology and medicine, John C. Eccles, asserts, "In some mysterious way, God is the creator of all living forms and particularly in human persons ... each with conscious selfhood of an immortal soul."[13]

And astronomer Owen Gingerich states flatly, "Just as I believe the book of scripture illuminates the path to God, so I believe the book of nature, with its astonishing details ... a blade of grass or the resonance levels of the carbon atom, also suggest a God of purpose ... a God of design." [14]

How Big is Heaven?

Although we know that heaven is above us, mere humans are incapable of grasping the infinite, so the size and scope of heaven itself must remain as elusive as our astronomical search for the edges and ends of the universe. In Jeremiah 51:15 (KJV), we are told: "He hath made the earth by His power; He hath established the world by His wisdom, and hath stretched out the heaven by His understanding." As we read in Job: "Lo, these are parts of his ways; but how little a portion is heard of Him? But the thunder of His power, who can understand?"[15]

Isaiah 42:5 (KJV) confirms: "Thus saith God the Lord, He that created the heavens and stretched them out; He that spread forth the earth, and that which cometh out of it; He that giveth bread unto the people upon it, and spirit to them that walk within."

In other words, heaven is infinite, as spread out as it pleases God, and way beyond our poor, limited, human imagination.

END NOTES

1. "And he left off talking with him, and God went up from Abraham" (Genesis 17:22).

2. "And no man hath ascended up to heaven, but he that came down from heaven, even the Son of man which is in heaven" (John 3:13).

3. "And when he had spoken these things, while they beheld, he was taken up, and a cloud received him out of their sight" (Acts 1:9).

4. "Let that day be darkness; let not God regard it from above, neither let the light shine upon it" (Job 3:4).

5. It is not in heaven, that thou shouldest say, Who shall go up for us to heaven, and bring it unto us, that we may hear it, and do it?" (Deuteronomy 30:12).

6. From an interview with Dr. R.C. Sproul, *The Evidence for Heaven* by Producer David W. Balsiger, Supervising Producer Charles, E. Sellier, and Executive Producers Don and Carol Scifres, Grizzly Adams Productions, Inc., Baker, Oregon, 2004. Dr. Sproul is the founder of Ligonier Ministries in Orlando, Florida.
7. From an interview by Tim Sheets, *The Evidence for Heaven* by Producer David W.

Balsiger, Supervising Producer Charles, E. Sellier, and Executive Producers Don and Carol Scifres, Grizzly Adams Productions, Inc., Baker, Oregon, 2004. Sheets is the author of *Heaven Made Real,* Destiny Image Publishers, Shippensburg, Pennsylvania, 1996.

8. From an interview with Michael Sabom, M.D., *The Evidence for Heaven* by Producer David W. Balsiger, Supervising Producer Charles, E. Sellier, and Executive Producers Don and Carol Scifres, Grizzly Adams Productions, Inc., Baker, Oregon, 2004. Dr. Sabom is the author of *Light & Death – One Doctor's Fascinating Account of Near-Death Experiences,* Zondervan Publishing House, Grand Rapids, Michigan, 1998.

9. From an interview with Ralph Muncaster, *The Evidence for Heaven* by Producer David W. Balsiger, Supervising Producer Charles, E. Sellier, and Executive Producers Don and Carol Scifres, Grizzly Adams Productions, Inc., Baker, Oregon, 2004. Muncaster is the author of *Going to Heaven,* Harvest House Publishers, Eugene, Oregon, 2001.

10. From *The Evidence for Heaven* by Producer David W. Balsiger, Supervising Producer Charles, E. Sellier, and Executive Producers Don and Carol Scifres, Grizzly Adams Productions, Inc., Baker, Oregon, 2004. Dr. Stephen W. Hawking is the author of *The*

Theory of Everything – The Origin and Fate of the Universe (from which the notes were made), *A Brief History of Time, Black Holes and Baby Universes and Other Essays*. He is the Lucasian Professor of Mathematics at Gonville and Caius College in Britain.

11. Excerpted quote from *The Evidence for Heaven* by Producer David W. Balsiger, Supervising Producer Charles, E. Sellier, and Executive Producers Don and Carol Scifres, Grizzly Adams Productions, Inc., Baker, Oregon, 2004. Monastery is the author of *Going to Heaven,* Harvest House Publishers, Eugene, Oregon, 2001.

12. Ibid.

13. Ibid.

14. Ibid.

15. "Lo, these are parts of his ways: but how little a portion is heard of him? But the thunder of his power who can understand?" (Job 26:14).

Heaven in Other Religions, Other Cultures, Other Times 7

"He answered and said unto them, Because it is given unto you to know the mysteries of the Kingdom of heaven, but to them it is not given" (Matthew 13:11 KJV).

In the search for evidence for heaven, it is necessary to note that not all people on the planet are Christians. But as defense lawyers look for corroborating evidence as they build credible, airtight cases, a look at some of the world's major religions gives us a picture of heaven that is amazingly consistent across theological and cultural lines. And even though we might call heaven by different names or interpret afterlife in different words, astonishingly, we are basically all describing the same thing.

According to the Bible, Heaven is the final destination for everyone who puts their trust in Jesus Christ as their personal Lord and Savior. Let's examine how non-Christian religions interpret the afterlife.

Judaism

As with most religions, there are disparate beliefs within Judaism, so describing the concepts of afterlife is difficult. In fact, some Jews do not believe in the afterlife at all. What is true for one sect—or in one tradition or for one era—is not true for all. Therefore, we will merely cover a few general concepts with the clear understanding that we mean to neither offend nor misrepresent. We are merely exploring a few ideas that appear or have appeared somewhere within the Jewish or Hebraic traditions.

Because Judaism is a covenant relationship between God and His chosen people that centers on agreements and fulfillments during life, the concept of an afterlife could be considered nearly inconsequential.

The ancient Hebrews described the universe in three tiers: heaven occupied by God and angels, earth occupied by living people, and an underworld (*She'ol*) occupied by the spirits of the dead. There was little need for detail, because life was centered on the "here and now" (or more accurately, the "there and then"), and the fulfillment of promises made by God during life. Interestingly, when promises were not kept (and many were not), theologians of the time considered the possibilities of resurrection after final judgment, a notion introduced by the Persians. There would be reward, just not in *this* life.

Of course, to be rewarded by being lifted to heaven means that there is judgment in someone's favor. But what if judgment is not favorable or is questionable? Then the soul descends to the underworld (She'ol), where it is purified for at least eleven months. This is why memorial prayers, called the Kaddish, are recited for exactly eleven months ... just in case someone's soul is retained for purification. By the way, if this sounds familiar, it is because this is likely the source of the notion of "purgatory"—neither heaven nor hell, but merely a sort of "holding tank."

Muslim

In the Muslim traditions, death is rest until the day of resurrection, when Allah will judge everyone. On that day, righteous Muslims are rewarded and unrighteous Muslims are punished. Non-Muslims might be judged favorably, but not until they have been purified in the fires of a form of purgatory.

Within Islam, there are two distinct Muslim traditions: the Shiites and the Sunnis. The Shiites believe that the soul uses the body, but when the body dies, the soul is liberated and can return to its truest nature, no longer encumbered. Those who believe in Allah may rest with Allah until resurrection. On that day, those souls rejoin their physical bodies and ascend to heaven. Non-believers are not afforded the period of rest after death. They suffer, are rejoined to the physical bodies, and then suffer eternal damnation.

Sunnis, on the other hand, believe that body and soul are united. When death occurs, the body and soul (one entity) are put into the grave, where they are judged together. A second death follows, but is formally abolished for those who died in the name of Allah (hence, the honor and purpose of terrorists' suicide missions in the name of Allah). Souls vanish and reappear on a day of judgment, when they rejoin their original bodies.

According to some Islamic traditions, Muhammad ascended into heaven with the archangel Gabriel. He went through the seven layers of heaven, up a ladder of light that all people see as they die. In the first heaven is Adam. In the second, Jesus Christ and John the Baptist. In the third, Joseph. In the fourth, Enoch. In the fifth, Aaron. In the sixth, Moses. And in the seventh, Abraham. Muhammad has direct interaction with each of these men—prophets like he.

Eventually, he travels above the seventh heaven to Paradise; he describes angels, tablets, and a throne. It is on this journey that Muhammad received the essential prayers that Muslims pray. Moses helped him pare the number of required prayers from forty to only five by boldly sending him back to Paradise repeatedly to ask that the number be reduced to something that his people could handle on a daily basis. After several concessions, Allah finally reduced the number to five. The Islamic concept of ascension to heaven and to Allah involves Christian prophets, and places Jesus Christ in a very low position.

Hindu

Hinduism tradition holds that the soul is an eternal self that is identical to and part of the cosmic Brahma—a transcendent and universal being: the "godhead." Although the soul does not change, it is trapped in a cycle of reincarnation: death and rebirth and death and rebirth. "Karma" is the determining factor in reincarnation and what the Hindus consider to be one of the universal laws, *Karma* states that for every action, there is a consequence. If you do a good deed, you are rewarded. If you do a bad deed, you are punished. If you do not reap reward or suffer punishment before your time on earth is up, then you must return to satisfy karmic law. Not only that, but the circumstances of your next birth are directly related to the reward or punishment, and the inescapable lessons you must learn. If one is a murderer in this life, the next life is going to be assuredly miserable. If one is saintly in this life, the next life might be an easier, privileged one.

Although there are varying traditions on breaking the cycle of karmic obligation, eventual freedom from having to return to life is their goal. This is supposedly achieved through virtue and insight. They believe the process can be accelerated through religious rituals and keenly attuned forms of advanced yoga that are designed to elevate consciousness.

So, what happens when the cycle is complete? According to their belief, the soul enters "mosksha." It returns to being in unity with the cosmic Brahma. The Hindus described this as bliss or *nirvana*.

In devotional Hinduism, Brahma is less "godhead" and more a loving God. Within this tradition, *mosksha* is not interpreted as a blending into the Brahma, but more as entering a tangible heaven where one may worship. They also have hell, where evil souls are tormented by demons. The Hindus believe hell is merely purgatory, a temporary imprisonment that inflicts torment and then returns the soul to the reincarnation cycle, no doubt relegating the soul to an unpleasant new incarnation, thus perpetuating the torment in order to teach some lesson and refine the spirit.

Buddhism

Buddhism is very similar to Hinduism in that it embraces *karma*, reincarnation, and the cycle of dying, then returning to life to learn and purify one's soul until achieving *nirvana*. Buddha thought that the purification to which one attains is achieved only when desire for things of this world is eliminated. Buddhism differs from Hinduism in its concept of soul. Rather than the eternal soul of a Hindu, the Buddhist soul is memory and character. And although a soul endures intact throughout life and death cycles, it's not eternal.

The *Tibetan Book of the Dead*[1] is a clear description of what the Tibetan Buddhist believes happens at death. When the body dies, according to Tibetan Buddhism, the spirit of the departed goes through a process lasting forty-nine days, following which it either enters *nirvana* (the goal) or returns to another body to gain the essential lessons required through living yet another cycle on earth. The first stage of the process is dying itself, where the person experiences a "clear white light"—the more spiritually advanced the person, the brighter the light and longer the experience.

The second stage is a sort of life review so vivid that the person might think he or she is actually living again. This is followed by encounters with deities and apparitions that reflect both the good and bad aspects of human nature.

Within Buddhism is the belief that there are levels of heaven and hell, including the life now being lived. Handling the encounters successfully is necessary for achieving *nirvana*. People who are highly evolved may not be subjected to this "testing;" rather, they may enter into a heavenly realm.

The third stage of the forty-nine day transition is reincarnation. This means failure to achieve *nirvana*, and the cruel realization that more refinement is in order. The spirit is put back on earth, born into another body, to experience, learn, and evolve, hoping that next time, things will be better.

Other countries

Researchers are amazed at the consistency of the evidence of an afterlife from all over the world. If one were tempted to surmise that stories have been passed across borders, so that mythology regarding afterlife and the existence of heaven have been "shared," then one would be wrong (or at least only slightly right). Even cultures that have had limited contact with the "outside" world report similar experiences and conclusions when we compare notes. Interpretations do vary, and cultural or religious nuances do influence the experiences, but for the most part, we are all telling the same story all over the world. We all agree. We have agreed since recorded time. There is an afterlife, and part of that is heaven.

From the Ancients

Speaking of "recorded time," it's significant that reports of the Near-Death Experience have surfaced in documents of antiquity.

While reports of Near-Death Experiences are by no means a recent phenomenon, societies are more aware of them because information is more easily accessible today than at any other time in history. The fact of the matter is that NDEs have been reported and recorded for thousands of years. Significantly, they are consistent with those seen today, but came from a time without mass media and the ability to instantly and globally share information and possibly influence perceptions. As today, reports of NDEs cross cultures and religions indiscriminately. We find accounts of NDEs in the Bible, the *Koran*, and the *Tibetan Book of the Dead*.

One of the most famous "classic" accounts comes from Plato, the Greek philosopher. In his book, *Republic*, he tells the story of Er, a solder who returned to life while on his funeral pyre and described what happened to him at death.

Er describes his soul departing and journeying with a great company, finding light of truth, and encountering a vision of pure celestial being and a vision of light. He also describes "judges" who directed his journey to the "righteous" or right opening, upward. (These same judges had directed the unjust to take the passage to the left, downward.) Er describes "delights and visions of a beauty beyond words." He specifically references bright, powerful, pure light. In other words, Plato describes a Near-Death Experience through the story of Er with accuracy and consistency that corroborate testimonials that are collected by researchers today.

Now, remember that Plato was not a Christian, so he had no preconceived notions of heaven from reading the Bible or seeing artists' renditions of heaven. Additionally, he was polytheistic. So, set against his theology that included Zeus and company, it's not surprising that his interpretation made no specific references to God. And yet, astonishingly, he describes perfectly "the light."

Later in *Phadrus*, Plato writes, "... the spectacles on which we gaze in the moment of final revelation; pure was the light that shone around us, and pure were we."

Plato wrote of it in his *Dialogues*: "We believe, do we not, that death is the separation of the soul from the body, and that the state of being dead is that in which the body is separated from the soul and the soul exists alone by itself?"[2]

Plato framed the question as a foregone conclusion. And the Bible, written and compiled over hundreds of years, contains many stories that suggest some people have had access to the world beyond. For example, in Acts 7:55-56 (NIV), Stephen has a pre-death vision. Surrounded by his enemies, Stephen cries out, "... I see Heaven open and the Son of Man standing at the right hand of God." And in 2 Corinthians 12:3-4 (NIV), Paul describes what many think was his own NDE: "And I know that this man—whether in the body or apart from the body I do not know, ... was caught up to Paradise. He heard inexpressible things, things that man is not permitted to tell." In this instance, could Paul have been telling us that he was actually there—in Paradise? What other evidence is there for such a place?

END NOTES

1. The *Tibetan Book of the Dead* is an ancient Buddhist guide for the dead and dying. The first part, Chikhai Bardo, describes the moment of death. The second part, Chonyid Bardo, deals with the states that supervene immediately after death. The third part, Sidpa Bardo, concerns the onset of the birth instinct and prenatal events.

2. Plato was a Greek philosopher who lived from 427-347 BCE. He was a student of Socrates. He is well known for passing along the Socratic style of thinking, and applying logic to abstract philosophical thought. His works include *Meno, Phaedo, The Republic, Phaedrus, Symposium, Theaetetus, Laws*, and *Timaeus*.

Evidence of Hell

"For if God spared not the angels that sinned, but cast them down to hell, and delivered them into chains of darkness, to be reserved unto judgment" (2 Peter 2:4 KJV).

Could it be that all these NDEs are actually describing heaven? And if they are, does proof of the existence of heaven, also prove the existence of its dark alternative—hell? Perhaps there's something to be gained from an examination of the life of a person caught up in *this* experience. What kind of lasting and significant changes take place in a person's life after such a traumatic event? Or does it just disappear into the forgotten shadows of memory?

Hell is not something people like to think about, much less talk about. But the existence of heaven, based on the readings of any Judeo-Christian writing, virtually guarantees the existence of its opposite domain, the fearful underworld Hades, the kingdom of the devil, commonly known as "Hell."

Hank Hanegraaff, author of *Counterfeit Revival*,[1] says, "Biblically, there's going to be the physical resurrection of all people. Some to eternal life. Some to eternal separation from God, His goodness, and His glory. And it is because that is what they choose.

In the Christian belief, we believe in heaven and hell, because without a hell, there would be no choice. God is neither a cosmic rapist who forces His love on people nor a cosmic puppeteer who forces people to love Him. Rather, God, the very personification of love, grants us choice. So people who have spent a whole lifetime distancing themselves from God are not, in the end, going to be involuntarily dragged into His presence for all eternity. If they were, heaven would not be heaven. Heaven, in fact, would be hell."

The discovery of heaven then is certain to confirm the existence of hell, a place that

Jesus describes in Luke 16. Jesus tells the story of a rich man who dies and is sent to hell. He looks up from hell, where he is in torment, and sees Abraham, far away. He begs Abraham to have pity on him, because he pleads, "I am tormented in this flame."[2]

We have heard of NDEs that relate to heaven, but are there any that relate to the dark side?

As a matter of fact, there are. Meet Howard Storm, author of *My Descent into Death and the Message of Love Which Brought Me Back*.[3]

Howard Storm had always considered himself to be a free thinker and an avowed atheist. He thought that belief in God was absurd. But a trip to Paris in 1985 changed all that.

Howard is an artist who was visiting the art museums and galleries of the famed City of Lights with his wife Beverly. They were on their last day of a European tour, and although it had already been a long day, he was excited to be concluding the trip on a much-anticipated high point: the Georges Pompidou Centre of Modern Art. They had saved the best for last.

He and his wife Beverly were in their hotel room getting ready, when suddenly Howard felt nausea rising in him, fully understandable on a whirlwind trip with unfamiliar food. It had happened occasionally. He took two aspirin and washed them down with stale Coke from the night before. But he had underestimated the problem. He was seized with abdominal pain so piercing that he dropped to the floor, screaming. He thought he had been shot. In fact, he frantically searched the front of his clothes, fully expecting to see blood. He scanned the room for the person with the gun. But there was no blood. No intruder. Only a wound that he couldn't see, but could definitely feel.

He screamed for his wife to call for help. Shocked and stunned with confusion, Beverly just stood and tried to make sense of what was happening. He screamed at her again. She ran to the phone, called the front desk and told them to summon a doctor immediately. In ten minutes a physician helped lift Howard from the floor to the bed, did an initial examination that confirmed alarming symptoms, and called for an ambulance.

Storm was diagnosed with a perforation in his small intestine. In a Paris hospital, his condition worsened. Believing without a doubt that he was near death, he said goodbye to his wife and slipped into unconsciousness.

As he tells it, "When I opened my eyes, I found myself sitting next to the bed, and thought to myself, 'This is impossible,' because moments before, I had been dying. Then I saw Beverly, my wife, sitting in the chair opposite me on the other side of the bed. I tried to talk to her, but she acted like she couldn't see me or hear me. No one could see me or hear me. And then I heard voices calling me from outside the room.

"These people outside the room were saying, 'Hurry up! Come with us! We've been waiting for you a long time! You've got to go now!'

"I thought they'd come to help me. I kept asking them who they were, but they just insisted that they had come for me; they were waiting for me; and it was time to go with them. So I thought they were to take me to my operation, and I went with them."

Storm describes the people as "male and female, tall and short, old and young adults. Their clothes were grey, and they were pale. I could never get more than ten feet from them. They wouldn't answer any of my questions, but kept insisting that I hurry. They promised that if I followed them, my troubles would end."

He followed this mob of people through encroaching darkness toward an unknown destination for reasons that were increasingly unclear. But one thing was for sure: They weren't going to the operating room. Storm's other realization was that these were not caring, nice people with his best interests at heart. They hurled insults at him and would answer no questions. Complete darkness engulfed them all. His growing sense of dread heightened, and in panic, he stopped.

"I wasn't going to go any further with these people, and I told them so. They started to push and pull at me, yelling and screaming at me. I fought back as hard as I could. There were dozens of them, maybe hundreds or thousands. There was no way to tell in that darkness. They were swarming all over me. The more I fought, the more vicious they became. To my horror, I realized that they were tearing me apart, consuming me. All of them were laughing and taunting me. And the more they hurt me, the better they liked it. As I lay there on the ground in the fetal position to protect myself from their kicks and taunting, I heard a voice say, 'Pray to God.'

"And I thought, 'I don't believe in God. How can I pray?'

"And a second time, it said, 'Pray to God.' And a third time.

"My prayer came out all mixed up with the 23rd Psalm, the Pledge of Allegiance, and the Lord's Prayer ... just little bits of them that I could remember. But the people around me hated any mention of God, and they were screaming at me. In my desperation, I yelled out into the darkness, 'Jesus, please save me!'

"With that, a tiny light appeared in the darkness, and became very bright, and came over me. It was the most brilliant, beautiful light that lifted me up and filled me with ecstasy. And I knew absolutely that this was the Jesus I had believed in as a child. He took me out of that horrible place that I now know was hell, and we began to approach heaven. With Jesus and the angels that He called over to us, we went over my life from the beginning to the end. And I was so ashamed of the things I had done in my life. But the important thing is that I knew that God loved me, and Jesus and the angels loved me in spite of the things that I had done.

"Eventually they told me that I had to come back into this world, which was almost unbearable to me—to be separated from them. But I knew that through their love for me and my love for them, I would never be separated from God or the heavenly beings or Jesus again."

As incredible as it sounds, Howard Storm remains convinced that it is real. In fact, that experience brought about a radical change in Howard's life, and transformed him from an unbelieving atheist to a committed believer. He credits that single event with causing a complete turn-around in his life.

He says of his experience, "I think the most important thing about NDEs is the way people's lives are changed. It has been studied by scientists and confirmed that people who've had NDEs lose their fear of death, but more importantly, they know that there's a governing love that rules the universe, and they want to be a part of it. Their lives are changed for the better—to be a part of that love."

Former atheist Howard entered United Theological Seminary and was ordained as a minister. He has been pastor of Zion United Church of Christ in Cincinnati since 1991. He has lectured on his personal experience in hell hundreds of times, and still becomes emotional when he speaks of being lifted by love.

Based on Howard Storm's experience, heaven's counterpart, hell, is equally real, but what of those whose experiences aren't as chilling as his? It's understandable that such a dramatic encounter with hell might change a person's life, but what happens when a person's experience is entirely different? What happens when the experience is strictly heavenly? Will that person also change?

END NOTES

1. From an interview with Hank Hanegraaff, *The Evidence for Heaven* by Producer David W. Balsiger, Supervising Producer Charles, E. Sellier, and Executive Producers Don and Carol Scifres, Grizzly Adams Productions, Inc., Baker, Oregon, 2004. Hanegraaff is the author *of The Counterfeit Revival*, Word Publishing, Dallas, Texas, 1997. He has also authored *The Bible Answer Book, The Covering, Christianity in Crisis, and the Prayer of Jesus.*

2. Luke 16:19-31
[19] There was a certain rich man, which was clothed in purple and fine linen, and fared sumptuously every day: [20] And there was a certain beggar named Lazarus, which was laid at his gate, full of sores, [21] And desiring to be

fed with the crumbs which fell from the rich man's table: moreover the dogs came and licked his sores. [22] And it came to pass, that the beggar died, and was carried by the angels into Abraham's bosom: the rich man also died, and was buried; [23] And in hell he lift up his eyes, being in torments, and seeth Abraham afar off, and Lazarus in his bosom. [24] And he cried and said, Father Abraham, have mercy on me, and send Lazarus, that he may dip the tip of his finger in water, and cool my tongue; for **I am tormented in this flame.** [25] But Abraham said, Son, remember that thou in thy lifetime receivedst thy good things, and likewise Lazarus evil things: but now he is comforted, and thou art tormented. [26] And beside all this, between us and you there is a great gulf fixed: so that they which would pass from hence to you cannot; neither can they pass to us, that would come from thence. [27] Then he said, I pray thee therefore, father, that thou wouldest send him to my father's house: [28] For I have five brethren; that he may testify unto them, lest they also come into this place of torment. [29] Abraham saith unto him, They have Moses and the prophets; let them hear them. [30] And he said, Nay, father Abraham: but if one went unto them from the dead, they will repent. [31] And he said unto him, If they hear not Moses and the prophets, neither will they be persuaded, though one rose from the dead.

3. From an interview with Howard Storm, *The Evidence for Heaven* by Producer David W. Balsiger, Supervising Producer Charles, E. Sellier, and Executive Producers Don and Carol Scifres, Grizzly Adams Productions, Inc., Baker, Oregon, 2004. Storm is the author of *My Descent Into Death – and the message of love which brought me back,* Clairview Books, Hammersmith, London, 2000.

Dannion Brinkley: Transformed by NDE 9

"Let your light so shine before men, that they may see your good works, and glorify your Father which is in heaven"
(Matthew 5:16 KJV).

The Near-Death Experience, by all evidence, is usually a "heavenly" one. Descriptions of tunnels, light, beings who greet and guide, and divine love notwithstanding, the majority of those who return from the brink of death come back with a resolute commitment to live better lives. Having witnessed the overwhelming and undeniable power of love and forgiveness, and having discovered with certainty that they are beloved children who play key roles in God's grand design, these people are forever changed.

It seems that a close encounter on the purely spiritual level with God is a catalyst for serious lifestyle decisions ... for the better. If the NDE didn't give a glimpse into "heaven," but in fact confirmed that there is no afterlife, that afterlife is neutral or even "hellish," then people who return from the brink of death would not resolve to lead more godly lives. They might assume "Carte Blanche" to run wild without responsibility or hope for their remaining years.

But this is not the case. On the contrary, Dr. Raymond Moody concludes that the subjects he's studied come back to follow a "God-directed" course. In order to trigger "God-directed" resolutions, the NDE must also, in fact, be "God-directed"—meaning directing the person toward heaven.[1]

One of the most famous stories of Near-Death Experiences is that of Dannion Brinkley. It's truly a story that begins with, "It was a dark and stormy night ...." He tells of his life-altering experience in his book, *Saved by the Light*.[2]

One night Dannion was talking to a friend on the phone from his bedroom in his home in Aikens, South Carolina. Warily watching the turbulent night beyond his window, Dannion paced nervously back and forth, having more and more trouble concentrating on the conversation. Deep thunder pounded the house, and lightning streaked down from black clouds, revealing strobe-light glimpses of relentless, torrential rain. Each rumble and flash made him flinch. Dannion had never been comfortable during thunderstorms and was anxious to get off the phone, wanting to get away from anything electric. He concluded his end of the conversation emphatically.

"Look, I've got to go. No, I just don't like thunderstorms."

But he was too late. He felt the hairs on his arm standing up as the room charged with the almost imperceptible, but unmistakable warning of an impending lightning strike. He didn't have time to consider the meaning of the odd sensation. Suddenly from the receiver of the phone, there was an explosion in his ear. Dannion was jerked literally out of his shoes and hurled back onto the bed. His body was shattered almost beyond recognition.

Dannion remembers leaving his body and watching as his wife Sandy tried frantically to keep him alive with CPR. Once, he dropped back into his tortured body, but not for long. Soon he was out again, watching the paramedics trying to save his life.

As the ambulance pulled away from his home, heading to the emergency room through the storm, Dannion Brinkley recounts his amazing transformation.

"There was the sound of chimes as the tunnel spiraled toward me and then around me. And then all of a sudden there was no Sandy crying. There were no paramedics working on me. There was no ambulance radio chatter. There was just me … and the tunnel.

"I looked ahead into the darkness. There was a light up there. I began to move toward it as quickly as possible. I was moving without legs, at a high rate of speed. Ahead the light became brighter and brighter until it overtook the darkness and it left me standing in a Paradise of brilliant light. It was the brightest light I had ever seen, but it was soothing to my eyes.

"I looked to my right, and I could see a silver form appearing like a silhouette through a mist. As it approached, I began to feel a deep sense of love that encompassed all the meanings of that word. It was as though I was seeing a lover, a mother, a best friend, in multiples a thousand-fold. This 'Being' engulfed me, and as it did, I began to experience my whole life, feeling and seeing everything that had ever happened to me.'"

Suddenly Dannion was at the hospital, looking down on the frantic scene in the emergency room. Medical personnel swarmed, rushing around him in an intense collective effort to find a spark of life, hoping to rekindle it. The paramedics in the ambulance had done their best to save him, but they had given up; and now as he watched, the doctors finally gave up, too. They pronounced him "dead," then gently slid a clean sheet up his lifeless body and over his face.

They pushed the gurney out into the hallway to await transport by an orderly. The next stop for Dannion was the morgue. Sandy, who had been waiting in the corridor with a family friend, fled in grief. The family friend walked slowly to the gurney to have a last moment with Dannion.

Then perhaps the most frightening part of the whole experience: Dannion was back in his body, under the sheet, and looking up through tortured eyes. He couldn't move or even make a noise, but he was very aware that his friend was standing next to him. The orderlies were on their way to take him to the morgue.

What's more, now that he was back in his body, it seemed that even his thoughts caused him pain. Dannion saw his friend's shadow through the sheet, and hoped that he would notice that he was alive. He did the only thing he could do to get his friend's attention. He blew on the sheet with a few short, shallow puffs. His friend saw the movement and excitedly summoned an orderly, who rushed Dannion back into the emergency room.

The body that Dannion came back to was horribly damaged. It would be months before he could move his arms or stand, let alone walk. But the experience would bring about a profound change in his life.

He says, "One of the most provocative points about the Near-Death Experience is that it begins to open up an understanding that there is a life after death. Not only is there life after death, but also there is a system by which we leave this world to enter that one. And the more we study that, the greater the opportunity to lift the veil, so that we know that there is not only this life, but also life after this one.

"From my personal experience, I know that there's life after death. Why? I've had three of these experiences—one death experience and two Near-Death Experiences: being struck by lightning in 1975 and declared clinically dead for 28 minutes, collapsing from heart failure and having to have emergency open-heart surgery in 1989, and then having emergency brain surgery in 1997—all complications from being struck by lightning. There is life after death, a wondrous, glorious place that awaits us.

"The Near-Death Experience begins to truly open the door, where science and medicine can begin to look at life after death. But personally, after going through three of these experiences, I'd like to say this. If you don't believe there's a life after death, you're missing the greatest part of your own life."

From that day to this, Dannion Brinkley has devoted his life to helping others. His Compassion in Action organization gives hope and understanding to hundreds each year. He's always on the go with his books, lecture tours, workshops, and assuring fellow humans that death is not an end and there is nothing to fear. Larry Dossey, MD, former Chief of Staff at the Humana Medical City in Dallas, says of him, "Brinkley's efforts have become widely known. He has recruited so many volunteers that he has single-handedly reinvigorated the hospice movement in the United States." By the way, Dannion has personally logged over 10,000 hours at bedside as a volunteer at Hospice. Clearly he returned from death to lead others.

For both Howard Storm and Dannion Brinkley, profound experiences with both heaven and hell brought about life-altering changes that drew them close to God, motivating them to share God's love and compassion with others. Having faced death and experienced the love and light, people return to their lives in a state of "conversion." Perhaps this is where the expression, "I saw the light," comes from when describing a truth revealed.

END NOTES

1. From an interview with Raymond Moody, M.D., *The Evidence for Heaven* by Producer David W. Balsiger, Supervising Producer Charles, E. Sellier, and Executive Producers Don and Carol Scifres, Grizzly Adams Productions, Inc., Baker, Oregon, 2004. Dr. Moody is the author of *Life After Life – The Investigation of a Phenomenon – Survival of Bodily Death,* Harper San Francisco (Harper Collins Publishers), 2000.

2. From an interview with Dannion Brinkley, *The Evidence for Heaven* by Producer David W. Balsiger, Supervising Producer Charles, E. Sellier, and Executive Producers Don and Carol

Scifres, Grizzly Adams Productions, Inc.,
Baker, Oregon, 2004. Dr. Brinkley is the
author (with Paul Perry) of *Saved by the Light
– The True Story of a Man Who Died Twice
and the Profound Revelations He Receive,*
Harper Collins Publishers, New York City,
New York, 1994.

A Word About Suicide and Heaven 10

"Most assuredly, I say to you, he who hears My word and believes in Him who sent Me has everlasting life, and shall not come into judgment, but has passed from death into life" (John 5:24 NKJV).

Some Christians view suicide as a mortal sin and therefore punishable by a sentence in hell. Some Christians view suicide as a tragic momentary lapse in judgment worthy of forgiveness. No one except God knows for sure, but there have been a number of Near-Death Experiences associated with attempted suicide that give us a glimpse into the few minutes that follow death. While the attempt to die appears to lead some to the light, in some cases, the NDE has been expressed as having been less than a good experience. In fact, some individuals who tried to take their own lives describe a descent into a murky hell. At the very least, to them the NDE was uncomfortable and confusing.

Sadly, it seems, the problems that drive these individuals to take their own lives do not diminish when they get to the other side. In fact, their despair deepens when they realize that not only are the problems still present, but now they have no way to "fix" all that is wrong. Once their physical bodies are disassociated, and they have no access to solutions, nothing can be corrected or made better.

Equally important, these individuals report that they regret the "hell" through which they put those who love them. "While the person who commits suicide dies only once, the loved ones left behind die a thousand deaths wondering why." The agony of a life so hard that it seems to require death in order to end the pain is now compounded by guilt and remorse. Combine those with frustration in knowing that nothing can be corrected, and one can probably get a good sense of hell without much effort or imagination.

As with NDEs not associated with suicide, sometimes there appears to be a "decision" point, where death is suddenly and deliberately averted, and the individual is sent back to life. In these cases, we observe the same positive changes in personality and character that accompany other NDEs ... and sometimes an amplified gratitude for second chances.

Some think that suicide is a violation of the sixth commandment, "You shall not murder" (Exodus 20:13 NKJV). Some think that suicide is the most heinous of all sins because one who takes his own life cannot repent of it. But what of eternal security—justification by grace, which Scripture clearly teaches?

"For by grace are ye saved through faith; and that not of yourselves: it is the gift of God: Not of works, lest any man should boast" (Ephesians 2:8-9 KJV).

Nothing can separate a Christian from the love of God. "For I am persuaded, that neither death, nor life, nor angels, nor principalities, nor powers, nor things present, nor things to come, nor height, nor depth, nor any other creature, shall be able to separate us from the love of God, which is in Christ Jesus our Lord." (Romans 8:38-39 NKJV).

"My sheep hear My voice, and I know them, and they follow Me. And I give them eternal life, and they shall never perish; neither shall anyone snatch them out of My hand. My Father, who has given them to Me, is greater than all; and no one is able to snatch them out of My Father's hand" (John 10:27-29 NKJV).

"And this is the testimony: that God has given us eternal life, and this life is in His Son. He who has the Son has life; he who does not have the Son of God does not have life. These things I have written to you who believe in the name of the Son of God, that you may know that you have eternal life, and that you may continue to believe in the name of the Son of God" (1 John 5:11-13 NKJV) .

Can suicide victims go to heaven?

Could a person who commits suicide be admitted to heaven—even though he has indeed taken a life and violated a critical commandment? Scripture certainly leads one to believe so. While none of us will ever *really* know, it's safe to assume that a person who commits suicide is mentally ill, under the influence of drugs, alcohol or extreme duress. By any measure, the person is either impaired—sick, if you will—or under conditions of severe stress, such as a soldier in battle who takes his own life rather than suffer painful torture or violent murder at the hand of a cruel enemy.

The questions of intention and clouded judgment certainly leave open the possibility that under "normal" circumstances, there would have been no suicide. In other words, suicide can be interpreted as a sort of accident—a mere attempt to stop or prevent pain that suddenly goes too far. Hell, in this interpretation, would be too harsh a "penalty" for a momentary lapse. There would be no reason to spend eternity within darkness. Heaven, indeed, could be the ultimate destination for a beloved child of God who has been assured salvation.

As for "freeing" a soul in anguish over the pain and guilt of having committed suicide (certainly a kind of hell by any interpretation), those left behind have the options of forgiveness and intercessory prayer. So, even if the death experience through suicide doesn't begin as a joyful journey into the light, perhaps it can be changed into one through love.

PART 3

From the Halls of Science: Research & Proof

Skeptics: Not Everyone Agrees 11

"And immediately Jesus stretched forth his hand, and caught him, and said unto him, O thou of little faith, wherefore didst thou doubt?" (Matthew 14:31 KJV).

Because our examples are taken from the Bible, Christian believers accept them as proof, but to the skeptics, they're merely more anecdotal evidence.

Skeptic magazine founding publisher and editor, Dr. Michael Shermer, says, "Outside of religion, there's no scientific evidence whatsoever of an afterlife or a place where any of us goes, other than in the ground—six feet under, pushing up daisies. That's the cold, hard evidence. It's unfortunate, but if we want to think of ourselves as living beyond, we have to do so through our work or through our children, but not through actual immortality."[1]

And, of course, there are those whose belief systems exclude any possibility of life beyond the grave. The skeptic finds no comfort in either the nature of the evidence or the amount of it. Gary Posner, MD, Contributing Editor, *Scientific Review of Alternative Medicine*, explains, "All of the commonly reported manifestations of these so-called Near-Death Experiences can be explained in either psychological terms or in terms of drug-induced or oxygen deprivation induced hallucinations, if you will. I can understand how someone inclined to believe in an afterlife and in heaven might interpret their experiences that way, whereas someone not oriented to that belief might be perfectly happy with a more normal explanation."[2]

But can these remarkable Near-Death Experiences be explained away simply as psychologically conditioned responses or hallucinations? There are some who disagree.

Sometimes skeptics attribute the Near-Death Experience as the hallucinatory effects of the brain shutting down when it's deprived of oxygen during clinical death. Just as many people describe the world getting darker and spinning around before they faint, some surmise that in the dying process, the brain shuts down systematically, one function at a time, and this produces physical sensations and hallucinations that are later described as Near-Death Experiences. The theory falters in studies that indicate that an NDE may occur before the body and brain begin to die physiologically. In fact, the person may be on life-support.

Dr. Ron Rhodes, author *Heaven, the Undiscovered Country: Exploring the Wonder of the Afterlife*, explains, "One of the medical explanations for Near-Death Experiences is called hypoxia. This has to do with the idea that when you die, the brain is deprived of oxygen. And that explains some of the feelings that you have, such as going through a dark tunnel and then seeing a bright light. However, one thing that that doesn't explain is the fact that people who go through a Near-Death Experience can typically recount with great detail what the doctors and nurses said, and the very specific procedures they went through in trying to save your life. So however you look at it, hypoxia and other medical explanations cannot account for that one fact."[3]

Skeptics suggest that Near-Death Experiences are induced by medications that are administered during medical crises. As a consequence, the patient experiences hallucinations, vivid dreams or psychotic delusions of leaving one's body that are interpreted later as being NDEs. In point of fact, there *are* some medications (such as ketamine) that do give the patient the impression that he or she has been lifted away from the body. For example, the patient might be fully conscious and yet unable to feel pain. The sedative effects of some medication can indeed cause a feeling of disassociation and an "I don't care" attitude. The experience can be described very accurately as "out of body."

But as similar as an "out of body" experience induced by medication and a Near-Death Experience are, they depart significantly on a couple of important points. First, many NDEs happen without medication in the equation at all. Or if medication is administered, it might not be known to induce hallucinations or affect the central nervous system in any way. The NDE is clearly demonstrated to be an event independent from a chemical standpoint. In fact, the person might not even be in the hospital or under the care of a medical professional at all. He or she might be alone in a car accident hundreds of miles from a hospital with a pharmacy.

Second, NDEs share a basic pattern that includes, among other things, bright light, a tunnel, a sensation of being pulled forward, beings or people to guide and greet, and peace and happiness. Experiences induced by medication vary widely from person to person, might be as vague and confused as any dream, and do not include any of the phenomena specifically associated with NDEs.

T. Lee Baumann, MD, author of *God at the Speed of Light*, says, "In my research I have found there to be no evidence that Near-Death phenomena are caused by either drug-induced hallucinations or psychological manifestations."[4]

Raymond Moody, MD, PhD, and author of *Life After Life*, says, "Having a doctorate in both philosophy and medicine, I think I'm a lot more attuned to some of the profound questions that these Near-Death Experiences raise for human consciousness. In short, I think it's over simplistic to say that these Near-Death Experiences can be accounted for simply as drugs, anoxia of the brain or by psychological factors."[5]

Once again the skeptics find themselves at odds with the experts, but if hypoxia and drug-induced hallucinations are the problem, then there's a lot of it going on. A Gallup Poll reports that eight million Americans (approximately five percent of the adult population) have had an NDE. In spite of the skeptics, researchers, continuing to build a growing body of impressive evidence, are far from being discouraged. While the search for heaven undoubtedly brings us face to face with the unknown and often the unexplainable, there are modern events that continue to provide us with strong evidence for the existence of heaven. Could it be that physicians and scientists can answer every question, refute every argument, and present the most compelling evidence for heaven for those who demand proof?

END NOTES

1. From an interview with Dr. Michael Schermer, *The Evidence for Heaven* by Producer David W. Balsiger, Supervising Producer Charles, E. Sellier, and Executive Producers Don and Carol Scifres, Grizzly Adams Productions, Inc., Baker, Oregon, 2004. Dr. Schermer is the Founding Publisher of *Skeptic* magazine, the Director of the Skeptics Society, a month columnist for *Scientific American*, the host of the Skeptics Lecture Series at Cal Tech, and co-host and producer of Fox television series, *Exploring the Unknown*.

2. From the notes of Gary Posner, M.D., interviewed for *The Evidence for Heaven* by Producer David W. Balsiger, Supervising Producer Charles, E. Sellier, and Executive Producers Don and Carol Scifres, Grizzly Adams Productions, Inc., Baker, Oregon, 2004. Dr. Posner is a Contributing Editor to *Scientific Review of Alternative Medicine*.

3. From an interview by Ron Rhodes, *The Evidence for Heaven* by Producer David W. Balsiger, Supervising Producer Charles, E. Sellier, and Executive Producers Don and Carol Scifres, Grizzly Adams Productions, Inc., Baker, Oregon, 2004. Rhodes is the author of *Heaven - The Undiscovered Country: Exploring the Wonder of the Afterlife,* Harvest House Publishers, Eugene, Oregon, 1996.

4. From an interview by T. Lee Baumann, M.D., *The Evidence for Heaven* by Producer David W. Balsiger, Supervising Producer Charles, E. Sellier, and Executive Producers Don and Carol Scifres, Grizzly Adams Productions, Inc., Baker, Oregon, 2004. Baumann is the author of *God at the Speed of Light,* A.R.E. Press, Virginia Beach, Virginia, 2001.

5. From an interview with Raymond Moody, M.D., *The Evidence for Heaven* by Producer David W. Balsiger, Supervising Producer Charles, E. Sellier, and Executive Producers Don and Carol Scifres, Grizzly Adams Productions, Inc., Baker, Oregon, 2004. Dr. Moody is the author of *Life After Life – The Investigation of a Phenomenon – Survival of Bodily Death,* Harper San Francisco (Harper Collins Publishers), 2000.

Logic, Science, and Faith 12

*"But I have prayed for thee, that thy faith
fail not: and when thou art converted,
strengthen thy brethren" (Luke 22:32 KJV).*

In science, there is a phenomenon known
as "empirical evidence." It means that you
experience or see something and draw
conclusions from it, rather than having to
prove it through repeated experimentation
that yields consistent results. A good example
is an apple on the table. How do you know
there's an apple on the table? You can see it
there. You may safely conclude, "Based on
empirical evidence, that apple is right there.
Period. End of discussion."

Empirical Conclusions from the Ancients: Third Heaven

The Hebrew ancients wrote of three distinct
heavens. First, they described air, the

atmosphere of gases that encases the earth. The second heaven they described was the firmament—that vast sky of stars, suns, moons and planets that we can all see on a clear, dark night.

The third heaven is the "heaven of Heavens, where God dwells." The Bible refers to the third heaven specifically. In 2 Corinthians 12:2 (KJV), Paul, speaking of himself, says: "I knew a man in Christ above fourteen years ago, (whether in the body, I cannot tell, or whether out of the body, I cannot tell, God knoweth;) such an one caught up to the third heaven." In Deuteronomy 10:14 (KJV): "Behold the heaven and the heaven of heavens is the Lord's thy God, the earth also, with all that therein is."

In searching for evidence for heaven and examining the Hebrew ancients' explanation of the three heavens, we can apply logic. We all agree that we breathe *air*, so we know that atmosphere is real. All we have to do is look up at night to be sure the *firmament* is real. Thus, we may infer logically that if the first two definitions of heavens are true and real (they got those right!), then the third is true and real, also, being the heaven of Heavens where the Eternal God dwells and which is spoken of, written about and attested to by myriads, from the earliest of men to the NDE survivors today.

Verifiable Experiences and Events

But faith in heaven cannot be a matter of logic, for Hebrews 11:1 (KJV) states, "Now faith is the substance of things hoped for, the evidence of things not seen." And although logic might seem to validate faith, the two are distinctly different, if not at odds with each other altogether.

Now, for validation, we turn to science: In order for something to be validated in science, the event has to be replicated and verified. For this to happen, all the details have to be reproduced and undergo rigorous testing for accuracy. All possible variables are controlled, and all possible explanations are examined for credibility or attribution. In other words, is this a pure experiment, replicated exactly as the same as the original event, and can the outcome be explained any other way?

Near-Death Experiences fall nicely into this validation model. They can be replicated, and are repeated so frequently that all possible variables are taken into consideration.

Faith and Science Merge

Can the mystery of heaven and the life hereafter only be found then through faith in God?

Dr. J.I. Packer, author of *Knowing Christianity*, says, "Without Jesus Christ, Son of God and Savior, there is no heaven for anyone. He is the Way, the Truth and the Life. In my experience, and I think in your experience, too, there's a longing for heaven deep in our hearts. No one longs for extinction. Everyone longs for fulfillment and happiness. I believe that this longing for fulfillment and happiness beyond this world is itself a pointer toward heaven, and everybody has it deep inside them.

"The religious beliefs of people do influence them, most definitely: both their belief about heaven and the reality of heaven for them."[1]

For the believer, the acceptance of heaven is a simple matter of faith. Scripture is clear on matters of heaven. Scientific proof then, while gratifying, isn't necessary to sustain that faith. But the non-believer, particularly one who relies heavily on intellect, may refuse to acknowledge heaven or even life after death without some credible proof touting, "Show me!" The medical community is starting to build a scientific case for the existence of an afterlife with these remarkable studies on Near-Death Experiences. But what other promising scientific research is going on?

As science searches for heaven, there is a possibility for an answer to the whole question of creation, not just the end of life, but also the beginning, as well. Is it possible to determine the validity of the anecdotal evidence? What do the worlds of physics, mathematics, and astronomy have to report about the possibility of life after death?

The evidence uncovered so far suggests not only an increasing level of awareness of the spiritual being in all of us, but a growing sense of the importance of that part of us. Due largely to the ability of modern medicine to resuscitate and sustain a failing body, literally "rescuing" people from death, an increasing number of people are bearing witness to life beyond the grave. As our search continues, a number of highly qualified researchers are trying to discover ways to demonstrate that these experiences are fact, not fantasy.

Some areas of psychological study still suggest that our cultural conditioning determines what we think about death and heaven. According to this line of reasoning, we interpret our experiences based on what we've been taught or our worldview. Could it be as simple as that?

Testing the NDE with Blind People Who See the Light

Dr. Kenneth Ring, author of *Lessons from the Light* and *Heading Toward Omega*, decided to tackle that notion head on. All people who report a Near-Death Experience remark on what they feel, hear, and see. But what if one of those sensations is completely missing from the earthly experience of the person reporting the NDE? What if the person is blind and has never seen the re-created images of the tunnel or the beings of light that pervade our culture's depiction of the NDE?

On the assumption that if cultural conditioning actually sets the stage, so to speak, for the clear and vivid visual images of an NDE, then a blind person, particularly someone who has been blind since birth, would have a very different experience. Dr. Ring reports, "I recently did a study in which I interviewed 31 persons, who were blind, about their Near-Death Experiences, including a number who were blind from birth. Eighty percent of these blind persons report being able to see, to see things of this world during their Near-Death encounters.

"When people talk about Near-Death Experiences and describe them in heavenly terms, they often talk about a realm of tremendous dazzling light, of supernatural beauty, and a feeling of total, unconditional acceptance and love. Having interviewed so many people about their Near-Death Experiences, I think one effect on me personally has been that it's made me feel a lot more comfortable about death. I think death is ... I won't say it's something to look forward to ... but I don't think we have anything to fear in the moment of death itself, however painful the process of dying may be."[2]

As Helen Keller said, "Death is no more than passing from one room into another, but there's a difference for me, you know. Because in that other room, I shall be able to see." She was right.

The Closer We Come to Death, the More Likely the NDE

Michael Sabom, MD and author of *Light and Death*, found that the closer a person comes to death, the more likely he or she is to report a Near-Death Experience, suggesting that the experience is part of a process that leads us progressively toward ... what? He says, "Again, I think the Near-Death Experience is a dying experience. It's not an after-death experience. These people are not going to heaven and hell, and coming back and telling us what it was like. I do think it's a powerful spiritual experience during the dying process. It's on the road, but it's not actually there. So it suggests that there's a spiritual realm that's leading somewhere, but exactly where is not what the Near-Death Experience is going to tell us."[3]

The Apostle Paul tells us that to be absent from the body is to be present with the Lord.[4] What's going to tell us where we're going, where heaven actually is, and how we go about getting there? Are Near-Death and out of body experiences the only tangible evidence of the road to heaven?

Dr. J.P. Moreland, author of *Immortality: The Other Side of Death*, concludes, "Besides NDEs, there are two pieces of evidence that indicate the reality of heaven. First, there is considerable evidence that God exists, and if God exists, then it's quite likely that there's an afterlife, because He would not create people and then snuff them out of existence. Second, there is solid historical evidence that Jesus of Nazareth actually arose bodily from the dead. If that is historical fact, as I believe the evidence indicates, then He has been to the afterlife and come back and told us what it's like. He can speak with authority, therefore, because He has actually seen it, since He rose from the dead Himself."[5]

Keith Harris, author of *The Unveiling*, agrees, "The most provocative evidence that we have that there is a heaven is what God's Word says about it. Heaven cannot be proved scientifically, so we have to have faith in what God says in His Word."[6]

Can Science Support Faith?

From the Christian point of view, of course, faith is the most important factor, but accepting that, what about scientific progress? What kind of interest is there in the scientific community? It may come as a surprise to many that from the late 17th century until today, there have been many highly respected scientists who have been working to prove that immortality is a natural physical phenomenon, and its study is, in fact, a branch of physics. J.J. Thompson, who discovered the electron, is among that group, as is Thomas Alva Edison.

One of the world's lesser known, but prolific scientists and inventors, a man by the name of George W. Meek,[7] gave up a highly profitable career and sold most of his businesses to pursue his quest for the possibility of a life hereafter. Long recognized as a brilliant American scientist and inventor with scores of industrial patents, George Meek retired at age 60, and began 25 years of intensive research into life after death. He traveled the world to locate and establish research projects with top medical doctors, psychiatrists, physicists, biochemists, ministers, priests, and rabbis. In 1987, he published the conclusions of his quarter of a century of research: "For the first time in 8,000 years of recorded history, it can now be said with certainty that our mind, memory, personality and soul will survive physical death."

END NOTES

1. From an interview with Dr. J.I. Packer, *The Evidence for Heaven* by Producer David W. Balsiger, Supervising Producer Charles, E. Sellier, and Executive Producers Don and Carol Scifres, Grizzly Adams Productions, Inc., Baker, Oregon, 2004. Dr. Packer is the author of *Knowing Christianity*.

2. From an interview by Kenneth Ring, Ph.D, *The Evidence for Heaven* by Producer David W. Balsiger, Supervising Producer Charles, E. Sellier, and Executive Producers Don and Carol

Scifres, Grizzly Adams Productions, Inc., Baker, Oregon, 2004.
Dr. Ring is author of *Lessons From the Light – What we can learn from the near-death experience,* Moment Point Press, Portsmouth, New Hampshire, 1998. Dr. Ring is Professor Emeritus of Psychology at the University of Connecticut and co-founder and past president of the International Association for Near-Death Studies.

3. From an interview with Michael Sabom, M.D., *The Evidence for Heaven* by Producer David W. Balsiger, Supervising Producer Charles, E. Sellier, and Executive Producers Don and Carol Scifres, Grizzly Adams Productions, Inc., Baker, Oregon, 2004. Dr. Sabom is the author of *Light & Death – One Doctor's Fascinating Account of Near-Death Experiences,* Zondervan Publishing House, Grand Rapids, Michigan, 1998.

4. "Therefore we are always confident, knowing that, whilst we are at home in the body, we are absent from the Lord: (For we walk by faith, not by sight:) We are confident, I say, and willing rather to be absent from the body, and to be present with the Lord" (2 Corinthians 5:6-8).

5. From an interview with Dr. J.P. Moreland, *The Evidence for Heaven* by Producer David W. Balsiger, Supervising Producer Charles, E.

Sellier, and Executive Producers Don and Carol
Scifres, Grizzly Adams Productions, Inc.,
Baker, Oregon, 2004. Dr. Moreland is a
Professor of Philosophy at Bible University and
one of the authors of *Immortality: The Other
Side of Death*, Thomas Nelson, 1992.
Moreland is The Distinguished Professor of
Philosophy at Talbot School of Theology, Biola
University, in La Mirada, California.

6. From an interview with Keith Harris, *The
Evidence for Heaven* by Producer David W.
Balsiger, Supervising Producer Charles, E.
Sellier, and Executive Producers Don and Carol
Scifres, Grizzly Adams Productions, Inc.,
Baker, Oregon, 2004. Harris has authored *The
Unveiling: A Journey Through the Book of
Revelation*.

7. Excerpted notes from *The Evidence for
Heaven* by Producer David W. Balsiger,
Supervising Producer Charles, E. Sellier, and
Executive Producers Don and Carol Scifres,
Grizzly Adams Productions, Inc., Baker,
Oregon, 2004. George W. Meek was the
founder of the Metascience Foundation, an
engineer and entrepreneur who made his
fortune in air-conditioning. At age 60, he
began traveling the world to explore spiritual
truths. He returned to form the Foundation,
which studied heaven, hell, the existence of the
human spirit, and healing.

Children and Heaven 13

"... Verily I say unto you, Except ye be converted, and become as little children, ye shall not enter into the kingdom of heaven" (Matthew 18:3 KJV).

Whether heaven is right next door or beyond our gaze, somewhere out there in the sky, we can be sure it's there. If, for example, it's been proven, as George Meek suggests, that we live on after physical death, the clear implication is that there must be a place—geography for heaven. Could it be that we must become "as a little child" to find it?

"... Let the little children come to me, and do not forbid them; for such is the Kingdom of Heaven" (Matthew 19:14 NKJV).

The Bible describes heaven as a place of incomprehensible splendor, a place He has prepared for those who have believed on His Son. Could it be, as some have suggested, that it's just a matter of cultural conditioning, an attempt to prove what's already believed? While the anecdotal evidence for a literal heaven continues to mount, research has turned to those least likely to be subject to cultural conditioning—children.

Melvin Morse, MD,[1] a leading world authority on dying children, describes himself as being an arrogant critical care physician with an emotional bias against anything spiritual. But that was before he began a series of scientifically based studies of dying children. He found that many others had already arrived at the conclusions he would soon reach. "When I review the medical literature, I think it points clearly to scientific evidence that something survives human death. This evidence includes case reports, reviews of the existing scientific literature, as well as direct experimental evidence—all causing a growing body of evidence in the scientific community, making it respectable to speculate that something survives human death."

It makes good sense to turn to children in examining death through Near-Death Experiences, because they have very little or no experience from which to draw in forming preconceived ideas about death or an afterlife. In fact, up until about age six, children have no conscious knowledge that death, as adults know it, exists at all (unless a friend, family member, or pet dies, and someone carefully explains this part of life).

Meet Katie

Katie, a small girl, fell into a YMCA pool and drowned. No one knew for certain how long she had been floating facedown in the water. Some speculated that she fell in. Some speculated that she might have been pushed. Others thought maybe she hit her head on the bottom. Dr. Morse considered the possibility of a seizure while she was in the water. No one knows for sure, and it's not important. What is important is that Dr. Morse was on the team in the emergency room when she was brought in. The battle to revive and save her was fierce and waged with only the smallest hope of success. As he would later write, "... she was a train wreck."

Dr. Morse says, "I was looking down at her lifeless body, wondering if there was any way that she could be saved. The CAT scan showed massive swelling of the brain; no gag reflex; and an artificial lung machine was breathing for her. Then the family came into the room and asked if they could pray for her. I thought that they didn't understand that she was certain to die. They held hands around her bed and they began to pray. Three days later, Katie made a full recovery.

"So not long after her remarkable recovery, she came to see me for a follow-up examination."

Into Dr. Morse's office walked a bright eyed, pretty, shy, little girl. She exhibited *none* of the telltale symptoms of being revived from drowning—no neurological deficits, no abnormal walk or mannerisms. Her intelligence appeared to be undiminished in any way by oxygen deprivation.

Her physical condition was not the only astonishing aspect of her recovery. What followed next would change Dr. Morse's life forever.

He says, "She clearly remembered my resuscitating her. In fact, I was amazed at what she could remember."

Katie stunned Dr. Morse by identifying not only him, but a physician who had been working with him, as well. She even knew which one of them had come into the room first. She was able to graphically describe medical procedures through which she had been unconscious. Not only was she able to recall details of the emergency room a few days before, but Dr. Morse says, "I remember very clearly that throughout her resuscitation, her eyes were closed. In fact, she was profoundly comatose the entire time that we were working on her. And I thought to myself, 'What is going on here?'"

His curiosity fully piqued, Dr. Morse asked her what she remembered about being in the swimming pool. Her answer gave him another shock. She innocently asked, "You mean when I met Jesus and the Heavenly Father?"

Dr. Morse said, "She didn't say anything more at the time. Maybe it was the shocked look on my face. Maybe she was embarrassed. But I brought her back for a follow-up interview, and at that time, she told me more of the details about when she was taken up to heaven."

Katie described a tunnel through which came a woman named Elizabeth, who accompanied her back through the tunnel herself. She saw her late grandfather and met some other people. At one point, she was allowed to wander through her home, to watch her siblings at play, her mother cooking dinner, and her father sitting in the living room, presumably worrying about her in the hospital. When Katie had disclosed this part of her adventure to her parents, they were shocked that she was able to describe the games her brother and sister were playing, the meal her mother was preparing, and her father's location in the living room and his demeanor. She had even described their clothing. She was accurate in every detail.

After visiting her home, Elizabeth, assumed to be a guardian angel, took Katie to meet the Heavenly Father and Jesus.

Dr. Morse recounts, "She said that Jesus told her that it was time for her to go home. And she said, 'No, I want to stay here in heaven. I'm having fun!'"

At this point in his story, Dr. Morse's eyes widen, he grins and continues, "And He then asked her, 'But don't you want to see your mother?' And at that point, she returned to what we call *consciousness*."

Dr. Morse addresses the possibility of Katie's story having been influenced by preconceived notions of heaven: "Katie came from a deeply religious family. They had a well-developed belief structure about death. But here's what's fascinating. Her experience was not really at all like what her family and religious training would have led us to believe would occur.

"For example, she went down a tunnel to heaven ... a tunnel that was lined with brightly colored bricks. But her family believes that when you die, it's like going to the edge of a river. The person who dies can go beyond the river and the rest of us wait on the shore. So if a Near-Death Experience merely reflects a person's cultural base, why wasn't that belief ... the river ... reflected in her dying experience? It didn't happen. There were unique elements in her experience that are not found in her family's religious belief system."

Dr. Morse published a report on Katie's Near-Death Experience in the *American Journal of Diseases of Children* in 1983. It was the first time any physician had done such a thing. Having been published and being a busy physician, he almost walked away from further inquiry. But then he recalled the fascinating work of Dr. Raymond Moody—especially his second book, *Reflections on Life After Life*. In that book, Dr. Moody had thrown down the gauntlet with his conviction that the Near-Death Experience is universal to all human beings.

"Dr. Morse began to wonder if children, without "cultural pollution," have experiences different from those of adults. It was an intriguing question ... and one that just might unlock the answer to "What happens after we die?"

Dr. Morse's research began simply. He says, "Our research in Seattle was designed to demonstrate whether Near-Death Experiences were caused by a lack of oxygen to the brain, some physiological derangement of the brain in the dying process or whether these were real experiences that truly happen to people when they die. And our results were nothing less than spectacular."

He wondered if children who had been life-threateningly ill (to the "brink" of death) might describe the same experience as children who actually experienced cardiac arrested. To find out, he interviewed children in both camps. He found children who had been on the same drugs as Katie, in order to replicate the possible effects of medication inducing "hallucination." He also found children who had nearly died and had been resuscitated. His interview was carefully designed to refrain from "leading" the kids into describing the NDE.

"We found that virtually all survivors of cardiac arrest had Near-Death Experiences, whereas our control patients who also had a lack of oxygen to the brain, who also were treated with various drugs, who also were resuscitated, but simply weren't near death ... those patients didn't have the experience. This led us to the conclusion that it takes coming to the point of death to create the Near-Death Experience, and it's not caused by drugs or lack of oxygen to the brain or hallucinations that are suffered during the dying experience."

None of the children with life-threatening illnesses and strong medications described the light or the tunnel or any of the phenomena associated with NDE. On the other hand, almost all of those children who actually "died" had at least one of the NDE experiences: leaving their bodies, seeing the light, traveling up the tunnel, meeting "dead" people, seeing a Being of Light, and having their lives reviewed. Some even admitted having made conscious decisions to re-enter their bodies and return to the "living."

Interestingly, all were a bit confused, most admitted that they didn't understand what had happened, and most had not told anyone —not even their parents. For some, their return to life had brought a new maturity and sense of purpose. The results of the research left no doubt.

Dr. Morse says, "Near-Death research, especially in children, gives us insight into what we call "heaven." It's clear that heaven isn't some sort of physical place, south of Jupiter, where we go when we die. Rather, it's a spiritual metaphor that comes to us when we die in ways that we can understand. That helps us to learn whatever lessons we're supposed to learn during the dying process."

Clearly to Dr. Morse, the Near-Death Experience is not caused by medications that can trigger hallucinations. The NDE is a natural part of the dying process. And the NDE is universal. Children who have "died" corroborate its validity as they relate the same story over and over and over.

Did Katie actually get a glimpse of heaven? Did she meet Jesus? Did they have a conversation that would urge Katie to decide to leave heaven and return to her mom? Few would argue that children like Katie have the capacity to make up such unique and detailed stories. Katie's experience certainly has similarities to the many other NDE stories, but unlike those of adults, hers unfolded through the inexperience and innocence of a child. Without bias and influence, Katie's Near-Death Experience and those of the children Dr. Morse has studied tell a truth that's hard to deny.

Do all or any of these NDEs bring us closer to a testimony of our own about the truth of heaven? Based on the testimony of those who say they have been there and come back, both heaven and hell are very real places.

In the meantime, various sciences are testing the concept of life after death, and the location of heaven against the theorems of quantum physics. While the most comprehensive and far-reaching of all modern studies states unequivocally that it can now be stated with certainty that life continues. The only question that remains is, "Will the evidence be believed?"

When Christ was on earth, He performed miracles in order to confirm who He was. He raised Lazarus from the dead. He changed water into wine with a touch. He healed those with leprosy, and brought sight to the blind. By the power of His Word, He calmed the storm and walked on the surface of the Sea of Galilee. In John 20:30-31 (NIV), we read, "Jesus did many other miraculous signs in the presence of his disciples which are not recorded in this book. But these are written that you may believe that Jesus is the Christ, the Son of God, and that by believing you may have life in his name."

END NOTES

1. From an interview with Melvin Morse, M.D., *The Evidence for Heaven* by Producer David W. Balsiger, Supervising Producer Charles, E. Sellier, and Executive Producers Don and Carol Scifres, Grizzly Adams Productions, Inc., Baker, Oregon, 2004. Dr. Morse is the author (with Paul Perry) of *Where God Lives,* Cliff Street Books (Imprint of Harper Collins Publishers), New York City, New York, 2000; and *Closer to the Light,* Villard Books, (Division of Random House), New York City, New York, 1990.

Scientists Join the Search for Evidence for Heaven   14

"For therein is the righteousness of God revealed from faith to faith: as it is written, The just shall live by faith" (Romans 1:17 KJV).

But even if, as George Meek insists, we can now say with certainty that there is life beyond this one, where does that take us on our search if science is at last willing to light the way? Can we find additional evidence for a place called "heaven?" Could it be that we're closer to our lost loved ones than we realize? Has scientific evidence already been uncovered that points toward the other world? In a universe teeming with all kinds of interstellar activity, it seems odd that critics and skeptics still maintain that there's nothing out there except empty space, but then critics and skeptics have been known to be wrong.

Sir William Preece, Chief Engineer at Britain's Post Office, is remembered primarily for stating that Edison's electric lamp was a " ... completely idiotic idea." And he wasn't alone. Several professors, including Henry Morton who, just as Edison was about to demonstrate his electric light globe, stated, "... on behalf of science, Edison's experiments are a fraud on the public."

Scientific American, the *New York Times*, the *New York Herald*, and academics from the United States Army all heaped derision on the Wright Brothers, claiming that it was scientifically impossible for machines to fly.

Prior to Christopher Columbus, experts believed the world was flat.

And even in a more sophisticated world, many skeptics still didn't "get it." Too many of them even to count stated that it was ridiculous to suggest that television waves could produce a picture. Historically, someone inevitably comes along to puncture the balloon of scholarly consensus. Given that reality, could it be that we've been looking for heaven in the wrong place? Is it possible that answers about heaven can be found in a physics class? Which brings us to a point in our investigation to which few people ever get, simply because the language of physics is often difficult to understand. But according to Dr. Melvin Morse,[1] there are physicists who are attempting to bring the discussion down to a more understandable level.

Physics and Faith

He says, "In England today, a group of scientists, mathematicians and university professors are working with subatomic particles and mathematical calculations which they believe could confirm that so-called "deceased" entities, although composed of different atomic components, exist in and share the same space with this material world."

Perhaps the most important question is, "Can these scientists, through physics, confirm the existence of the individual soul?"

Dr. Fred Wolf, author of *The Spiritual Universe*, says, "I believe there is proof that the soul exists. Quantum physics itself indicates the existence of another realm—a realm we might say is the realm of the soul. And it indicates that consciousness itself is something outside of just the mere body."[2]

Well, that's certainly an interesting concept and it might challenge some of our traditional thinking, but the important questions are: "Does it square with biblical truth?" How does the Bible correlate with the new physics? Can it be reconciled with the scientific view?" Interestingly, Dr. Tim Sheets thinks it can.

He says, "Particle physics tells us that there are possibly 11 different dimensions. When Jesus appeared to His disciples in Luke 24,[3] He appeared to them in a closed up room, and yet He had flesh and He had bone. He could eat and drink. How did He do that? Well, we're told that would occur in the sixth dimension. Evidently in a glorified body, dimensions are increased. There's a release from our dimensions now—length, breadth, and height—and dimensions are multiplied. We are told that Jesus appearing to His disciples in a closed up room would happen in the sixth dimension. From the sixth dimension, you could eat an orange from the inside out."[4]

It seems that the Bible and science, much to the consternation of some skeptics, do confirm each other. Heaven could be just a step across the threshold into another whole new realm.

Could it be that God provides these scientific insights and NDEs to demonstrate that He is real? That heaven is real? And that through knowledge and experience, our faith can be strengthened? Dr. Raymond Moody, MD, PhD, thinks so. He says, "Many people with NDEs do tell us that they feel that God gave them this experience for a specific purpose—usually something that was going on in their lives. And some have also expressed the opinion that perhaps these things are divulged to human beings because God wants to certify for us or affirm that there is life after death."[5]

END NOTES

1. From an interview with Melvin Morse, M.D., *The Evidence for Heaven* by Producer David W. Balsiger, Supervising Producer Charles, E. Sellier, and Executive Producers Don and Carol Scifres, Grizzly Adams Productions, Inc., Baker, Oregon, 2004. Dr. Morse is the author (with Paul Perry) of *Where God Lives,* Cliff Street Books (Imprint of Harper Collins Publishers), New York City, New York, 2000; and *Closer to the Light,* Villard Books, (Division of Random House), New York City, New York, 1990.

2. From an interview with Dr. Fred Alan Wolf, *The Evidence for Heaven* by Producer David W. Balsiger, Supervising Producer Charles, E. Sellier, and Executive Producers Don and Carol Scifres, Grizzly Adams Productions, Inc., Baker, Oregon, 2004. Dr. Wolf is a physicist and author of *The Spiritual Universe: How Quantum Physics Proves the Existence of the Soul*, originally published by Simon and Schuster, 1996, Moment Point Press, Inc. Portsmouth, New Hampshire, 1999. His work includes bridging gaps between the science of quantum physics and shamanism, psychology, human behavior, and spirituality.

3. Luke 24:36-43

[36] And as they thus spake, Jesus himself stood in the midst of them, and saith unto them, Peace be unto you. [37] But they were terrified and affrighted, and supposed that they had seen a spirit. [38] And he said unto them, Why are ye troubled? and why do thoughts arise in your hearts? [39] Behold my hands and my feet, that it is I myself: handle me, and see; for a spirit hath not flesh and bones, as ye see me have. [40] And when he had thus spoken, he shewed them his hands and his feet. [41] And while they yet believed not for joy, and wondered, he said unto them, Have ye here any meat? [42] And they gave him a piece of a broiled fish, and of an honeycomb. [43] And he took it, and did eat before them.

4. From an interview by Dr. Tim Sheets, *The Evidence for Heaven* by Producer David W. Balsiger, Supervising Producer Charles, E. Sellier, and Executive Producers Don and Carol Scifres, Grizzly Adams Productions, Inc., Baker, Oregon, 2004
Sheets is the author of **Heaven Made Real,** Destiny Image Publishers, Shippensburg, Pennsylvania, 1996.

5. From an interview with Raymond Moody, M.D., *The Evidence for Heaven* by Producer David W. Balsiger, Supervising Producer

Charles, E. Sellier, and Executive Producers Don and Carol Scifres, Grizzly Adams Productions, Inc., Baker, Oregon, 2004. Dr. Moody is the author of *Life After Life – The Investigation of a Phenomenon – Survival of Bodily Death,* Harper San Francisco (Harper Collins Publishers), 2000.

God of Light 15

"The people which sat in darkness saw great light; and to them which sat in the region and shadow of death light is sprung up" (Matthew 4:16 KJV).

With God now in the picture as the author of that grand design, the discussion branches out into other scientific areas. For example, that branch of physics that holds to the theory of the "Big Bang." Can the idea of some unknown cosmic accident billions of years ago be reconciled with the notion of a universe that is the product of an elegant design? Not according to Oxford mathematician Roger Penrose who actually calculated the odds against the possible generation of life dating back to the inception of the so-called "Big Bang." His arithmetic reveals the staggering odds of one out of a billion billion billion repeated more than a billion billion times—in other words, a mathematical and statistical impossibility. So given that reality, is there anything that can bring the assurance of religion and the pragmatism of science together? Well, perhaps there is.

The galvanizing scientific discipline that binds science and God in unifying evidence is quantum physics.

In his book, *God at the Speed of Light*, T. Lee Baumann, MD, suggests that the key to proof might be found in light. He says, "In my research, I've tried to look closely at the latest information on NDE, at the latest thinking in quantum physics, and at new interpretations of information from the Bible, as well as the mysterious, fascinating nature of light."[1]

Other researchers, notably Drs. Moody and Morse, have found light to be the keynote event, the element that always leads to a transformation in their lives. But the question is, why light? Why not darkness? Physiologically, isn't death a descent into darkness? Yet Dannion Brinkley and almost all others who have experienced death, see light. Why?

The fact is, there is no rational explanation for this occurrence. Einstein, however, showed us in the flow of light the corollary with the eternal now. Today, more scientists are recognizing the significance of the electromagnetic radiation that pervades our daily lives ... including light.

Light is Conscious

Incredibly, physicists have performed experiments that even suggest that light is conscious. That is to say, in these experiments, light appears to be capable of making decisions. Physicists have gone so far as to term this a form of consciousness, and by that I mean, light appears to be capable of anticipating changes in experiments and altering its behavior accordingly.

Light is one of the defining elements of a Near-Death Experience, and so we are safe in assuming that it is equally characteristic of death—one step beyond. Researchers who have compiled anecdotal testimony on NDEs agree that not only do all people who have an NDE report the light, but it figures prominently in the experience, and often is cited as being the most transformational, influential aspect of having "been dead." This is a significant ranking in importance when one considers that one of the other elements of an NDE is reuniting with dead friends and relatives, presumably beloved and sorely missed. And yet the light is considered to be most important.

The Being of Light

It is fascinating, too, that individuals who experience the light attribute a personality to it. No one reports a beam of light or a shining "something." They report that the light is a "being," who radiates an inviting warmth and the greatest love they've ever felt.[2] There is no need for speaking; there is direct and pure communication without verbal exchange—a sort of instantaneous mental telepathy. They feel compelled to be drawn ever nearer to the light.

Cultures differ slightly on specifically identifying the "being." Some describe a guide as a sort of a veteran counselor who comes to lead the dying person to his or her final destination. Some describe a judge. Christians, of course, quickly recognize this "being" as Jesus Christ.

That death is associated with light makes no sense from a logical perspective. A dying person closes his eyes and enshrouds his field of vision in darkness. Also, as the brain begins the process of dying and shutting down, one would assume that all consciousness would "fade to black," as they say in the theater. In fact, when someone faints and loses consciousness, it is often described as "everything went black."

Not only that, but death in western culture is widely associated with black. Mourners wear black clothing or black armbands. And the ceremonial aspects of the funeral are also predominantly expressed in black: black hearses, black wreathes, black horses, etc. Clearly, our society has determined that the color of death is black. And yet amazingly, in descriptions of the Near-Death Experience, people describe the polar opposite. They describe light—the brightest they've ever known.

Defining Light

Before we ask ourselves, "Why light?", we need to ask, "What is light?" Here's where quantum physics comes into play, and we turn to Albert Einstein. He developed "The Theory of Relativity" early in the twentieth century and described the wondrous properties of light, changing the face of physics forever.

Light travels at 186,000 miles per second. No one disagrees with this. But after Einstein, scientists now know that light doesn't need a medium to travel, as opposed to sound, which requires a surface to create vibration that we can detect … or hear. At one time, physicists theorized that light needed to bounce off something in order to be seen. They thought there must be some sort of property to the space that air occupies: a void called "ether." They conducted elaborate experiments to try and demonstrate that light would move more slowly when it traveled with the rotation of the earth and encountered resistance against "ether," but when light was beamed across "ether" without resistance, it would travel faster. The experiment revealed a shocking, unbelievable, astonishing truth. Light traveled at the same speed, no matter how they beamed it or refracted it. Impossible! And yet absolutely true.

To put this into an easy-to-understand context, we once again compare light to sound. Unlike light, sound is variable according to direction and source. The farther you are from the sound, the less able you are to hear it. A whisper directly into your right ear is easier to hear than a spoken word 20 feet from behind you. In other words, sound changes. The conclusion of experimentation that unlike any other phenomenon in the universe, *light is unchanging*.

Einstein told us that as an object increases in speed and approaches the speed of light, it decreases in length and increases in mass. Time slows down in direct proportion to its speed. If the object reaches the speed of light, time stops. In fact, we know that all forms of magnetic radiation (light) are timeless. Astrophysicist John Gribbon describes an electromagnetic wave as being "everywhere along its path (everywhere in the universe) at once, or you can say that distance does not exist for an electromagnetic wave." So for light, there is no time or space. It's everywhere all the time: omnipresent and infinite.

But it gets better. It also appears that light has intelligence. In the famous "Double-Slit Experiment" or "Two-Slit Phenomenon Study" conducted in 1803 by Thomas Young (and since replicated many times over), light was passed through a narrow slit onto a screen. The result of that pass was a fuzzy, narrow blur on the screen. One would think that if the scientist passed two beams of light through two slits side by side, the result would be two fuzzy blurs that probably intersected somewhere in the middle. But one would be wrong. The light shows up on the screen as alternating bands of dark and light that look very much like a modern day bar code.

It gets even better. When the light is fired through the slits one photon at a time, it appears that a single photon can pass through two slits simultaneously to form the alternating bands of dark and light on the screen. If only the single slit is open, the photons appear in a single image without interference. But how does the light know how many slits are open? How can it interact or interfere with itself? The wonder of this mysterious, outrageous result is that it appears that the light assesses the situation and makes a decision regarding appropriately passing through the slit or slits ... and organizes itself accordingly on the screen on the other side. Photons, pure energy in the form of light, appear to be conscious, make choices, communicate somehow, influence each other and modify their behavior according to information they are provided.

Quantum physicists have replicated the results of the "Double-Slit Experiment" in a number of other ways. In fact, scientists have even devised ways of interfering with the photons' path, and the light outsmarts them! To dodge the sudden interference, light must move "faster" than the speed of light. No problem. In other words, light can be everywhere all the time.

Light Unifies
So how does this apply as evidence for heaven? Simple. Quantum physicists and

mathematicians build a credible case for light being the unifying force of the universe. Everywhere. All the time. No present. No past. No future. Intelligent. Knowing. As a person dies, we literally see the light go out of his eyes. Perhaps we now know where it goes. If, at the moment of death, a person merges or joins with the light that so many describe, might we not rightly conclude that the person (his own light) has joined the infinite and immortal God?

"If a relationship possibly exists between light and a supreme being, perhaps it manifests in ways that have already been revealed to those who, over the centuries, have been believers in God."[3]

Dr. Tim Sheets, author of *Heaven Made Real*, says, "Scripture abounds with references that are especially meaningful in this new context. In Psalms 104, we read, 'O Lord, my God, thou are very great. Thou art clothed with honor and majesty, who coverest thyself with light as with a garment.' John 8:12 (NRSV) says, 'Again, Jesus spoke to them, saying, I am the light of the world. He who follows me will not walk in darkness, but will have the light of life.' And in 1 John 1:5 (NIV), a clear testimony is given: 'This is the message we have heard from him and proclaim to you. That God is light and in him is no darkness at all.' This barely scratches the surface of both the Old and New Testament references concerning God manifesting Himself as light."[4]

The Bible is replete with light as power and function. The mystical Jewish text, known as the Kabbalah, tells us, "The light created by God in the act of creation was flared from one end of the universe to the other and was hidden away." Could it be that science, after all these years, is about to write a preamble to the book of Genesis?

Dr. T. Lee Baumann says, "My research would indicate that the common element for Near-Death [Experiences], for scientific research on light, for quantum physics in general is that *light is omnipotent, omniscient, omnipresent, and has a consciousness*. With those facts, which again have been scientifically proven, it appears conclusive to me that light and God are intimately associated. In summary, light represents the existence of God.

"From my research, it is my belief that God resides everywhere in the form of light."[5]

Scripture Verifies Science

Dr. Tim Sheets says, "The Scripture is full of references concerning God and light. And of course, heaven is filled with the light of God. When someone dies, it's not unusual for him or her to experience some kind of light, whether it's God appearing to them as some kind of light form, or seeing heaven itself in some kind of light form.

"The Scripture says in Revelation, the New Jerusalem doesn't need a sun or a moon because the Lamb of God ... or Jesus ... is the light thereof. Jesus has been glorified by Father God, and the light, or glory, or Jesus is very brilliant. Often when people die and see Jesus, they will describe him as being a being of great light.

"When we go to heaven, all three parts of our makeup ascend to the presence of God—the physical (the body), the mind, and the spirit. Of course, the physical part is changed. The Bible says we will be changed to be like Jesus, so the physical part is changed from the composition of flesh and bone and blood to flesh, bone and light."[6]

Although searching for evidence for heaven in a physicist's lab might seem an unlikely path to discovery, it does provide us with some frankly compelling evidence that even skeptics cannot deny: scientific data, which demonstrates that light is omnipresent, omniscient, omnipotent, and has a consciousness. Dr. T. Lee Baumann points out that even in total darkness and in a vacuum, for every cubic meter of space, there are over 400 million photons or light waves. In summary, light verifies the existence of God.

These startling epiphanies bear repeating: *Even in the darkness, even in a vacuum, there is omnipresent, omniscient, and omnipotent light. There is God.*

Albert Einstein proved the existence of God in heaven with his famous equation: E (energy) $= MC^2$ (M meaning mass).

Simplified, this means that all mass eventually will become pure energy ... or light.

So, what does that have to do with heaven? Could immortality be as simple as Einstein's equation? Is it possible that death is little more than converting human mass into pure energy and merging our light with the light of God? Is heaven a joining?

When people have NDEs, they often initially find themselves in darkness (which we now know is filled with light). Typically, they then see light. They find themselves in a tunnel and follow the light, which usually takes them to a being of light, typically identified as God, Christ, or some type of guide. The reports are consistent and many. From thousands of eyewitnesses who have been to the edge of death and returned to assure us, clearly, death isn't an ending; it's a portal to life in heaven, where we join with the light to be with God.

"At midday, O king, I saw in the way a light from heaven, above the brightness of the sun, shining round about me and them which journeyed with me" (Acts 26:13 KJV).

END NOTES

1. From an interview by T. Lee Baumann, M.D., *The Evidence for Heaven* by Producer David W. Balsiger, Supervising Producer Charles, E. Sellier, and Executive Producers Don and Carol Scifres, Grizzly Adams Productions, Inc., Baker, Oregon, 2004. Baumann is the author of *God at the Speed of Light*, A.R.E. Press, Virginia Beach, Virginia, 2001.

2. "This then is the message which we have heard of him, and declare unto you, that God is light, and in him is no darkness at all" (1 John 1:5).

3. From an interview by T. Lee Baumann, M.D., *The Evidence for Heaven* by Producer David W. Balsiger, Supervising Producer Charles, E. Sellier, and Executive Producers Don and Carol Scifres, Grizzly Adams Productions, Inc., Baker, Oregon, 2004. Baumann is the author of *God at the Speed of Light*, A.R.E. Press, Virginia Beach, Virginia, 2001.

4. From an interview by Dr. Tim Sheets, *The Evidence for Heaven* by Producer David W. Balsiger, Supervising Producer Charles, E. Sellier, and Executive Producers Don and Carol Scifres, Grizzly Adams Productions, Inc.,

Baker, Oregon, 2004. Sheets is the author of
Heaven Made Real, Destiny Image Publishers,
Shippensburg, Pennsylvania, 1996.

5. From an interview by T. Lee Baumann,
M.D., ***The Evidence for Heaven*** by Producer
David W. Balsiger, Supervising Producer
Charles, E. Sellier, and Executive Producers
Don and Carol Scifres, Grizzly Adams
Productions, Inc., Baker, Oregon, 2004.
Baumann is the author of ***God at the Speed of
Light,*** A.R.E. Press, Virginia Beach, Virginia,
2001.

"This then is the message which we have heard
of him, and declare unto you, that God is light,
and in him is no darkness at all" (1 John 1:5).

6. "He that loveth not knoweth not God; for
God is love" (1 John 4:8).

EPILOGUE

We trust that you enjoyed our special look at our evidence for heaven. Perhaps it's strengthened your faith, and even given you a greater understanding of heaven that will help you better share its reality with others.

Heaven is real. As one of our experts testified, perhaps it's more real than where we now stand. If heaven is real, then it's true that its dark alternative—hell—must also be real. Then perhaps the most important question of all: What is your eternal destiny and where you'll spend it? And the amazing fact is, it's your choice.

While we have explored heaven from several aspects (including quantum physics and surgically induced out-of-body experiences) and drawn inferences from Near-Death Experiences that have been described to us, the truth is that there is no tangible "evidence" for heaven. None is required. Heaven—all that we know—is a matter of faith. Simple faith.

*"Hold fast the form of sound words,
which thou hast heard of me, in faith
and love which is Christ Jesus"
(2 Timothy 1:13 KJV).*

Bibliography

If You Would Like to Read More

Baumann, T. Lee, M.D.
God at the Speed of Light
A.R.E. Press
Virginia Beach, Virginia, 2001

Blanchard, John
Whatever Happened to Hell?
Crossway Books
Wheaton, Illinois, 1995

Brinkley, Dannion
    with Paul Perry
*Saved by the Light – The True Story of a Man
Who Died Twice and the Profound
Revelations He Received*
Harper Collins Publishers
New York City, New York, 1994

Brown, Daniel A., Ph.D.
What the Bible Reveals About Heaven
Regal Books
Ventura, California, 1999

Buchanan, Alex
Heaven and Hell
Sovereign World Ltd.
Kent, England, 1995

Connelly, Douglas
The Promise of Heaven
InterVarsity Press
Downers Grove, Illinois, 2000

Cox-Chapman, Molly
The Case for Heaven
The Berkley Publishing Group
New York City, New York, 1995

Crockett, William, Editor
Four Views on Hell
Zondervan Publishing House
Grand Rapids, Michigan, 1992

Dixon, Larry
Heaven: Thinking Now About Forever
Christian Publications, Inc
Camp Hill, Pennsylvania, 2002

Ensley, Eddie
Visions - The Soul's Path to the Sacred
Loyola Press
Chicago, Illinois, 2000

Fernando, Ajith
Crucial Questions About Hell
Crossway Books
Wheaton, Illinois, 1999

Ford, Marvin
As told to Dave Balsiger and Don Tanner
On the Other Side
Logos International
Plainfield, New Jersey, 1978

Geisler, Norman and Brooks, Ron
When Skeptics Ask
Barker Books
Grand Rapids, Michigan, 1990

Habermas, Gary R. and Moreland, J. P.
Beyond Death – Exploring the Evidence for Immortality
Crossway Books
Wheaton, Illinois, 1998

Holding, Rafael
Hearing From Heaven - How It's Done
Aurora Production
Switzerland, 2000

Hunt, Dave
Whatever Happened to Heaven?
Harvest House Publisher
Eugene, Oregon, 1988

Jeffrey, Grant R.
Heaven - The Mystery of Angels
Frontier Research Publications
Toronto, Ontario, 1996

Jeffrey, Grant R.
Heaven - The Last Frontier
Frontier Research Publications
Toronto, Ontario, 1990

Lucado, Max
The Applause of Heaven
Word Publishing (A Thomas Nelson Company)
Nashville, Tennessee, 1999

Lutzer, Erwin W.
One Minute After You Die – A Preview of Your Final Destination
Moody Press
Chicago, Illinois, 1997

MacArthur, John F.
The Glory of Heaven
Crossway Books
Wheaton, Illinois, 1996

Moody, Raymond A., M.D.
Life After Life – The Investigation of a Phenomenon – Survival of Bodily Death
Harper San Francisco (Harper Collins Publishers), 2000

Morrow, Barry
Heaven Observed
NavPress
Colorado Springs, Colorado, 2001

Morse, Melvin, M.D.
  with Paul Perry
Where God Lives
Cliff Street Books (Imprint of Harper Collins
Publishers)
New York City, New York, 2000

Morse, Melvin, M.D.
  with Paul Perry
Closer to the Light
Villard Books, (Division of Random House)
New York City, New York, 1990

Muncaster, Ralph O.
Going to Heaven
Harvest House Publishers
Eugene, Oregon, 2001

Rhodes, Ron
*Heaven - The Undiscovered Country:
Exploring the Wonder of the Afterlife*
Harvest House Publishers
Eugene, Oregon, 1996

Ring, Kenneth, Ph.D.
*Lessons From the Light – What we can learn
from the near-death experience*
Moment Point Press
Portsmouth, New Hampshire, 1998

Rommer, Barbara R., M.D.
Blessing In Disguise – Another Side of the Near-Death Experience
Llewellyn Publications (A Division of Llewellyn Publications Worldwide, Ltd.)
St. Paul, Minnesota, 2000

Sabom, Michael, M.D.
Light & Death – One Doctor's Fascinating Account of Near-Death Experiences
Zondervan Publishing House
Grand Rapids, Michigan, 1998

Sheets, Tim
Heaven Made Real
Destiny Image Publishers
Shippensburg, Pennsylvania, 1996

Storm, Howard
My Descent Into Death – and the message of love which brought me back
Clairview Books
Hammersmith, London, 2000

Tada, Joni Eareckson
Heaven Your Real Home
Zondervan Publishing House
Grand Rapids, Michigan, 1995

Thomas, Choo
Heaven Is So Real
Creation House Press
Lake Mary, Florida, 2003

Wolf, Fred Alan, Ph.D.,
*The Spiritual Universe: How Quantum
Physics Proves the Existence of the Soul,*
originally published by Simon and Schuster,
1996, Moment Point Press, Inc.
Portsmouth, New Hampshire, 1999

DVD or VHS
Balsiger, David W. and Sellier, Charles, E.
Executive Producers Don and Carol Scifres
The Evidence for Heaven
Grizzly Adams Productions, Inc.
Baker, Oregon, 2004

VHS
Discovery Media Productions, Inc.
*Heaven & Hell – Biblical Images of the
Afterlife*
Distributed by Questar, Inc.
Chicago, Illinois, 1999

Lakewood Television
*Death & Beyond – A historical and spiritual
journey to uncover the truth about what
awaits us.*
Impact Production
Tulsa, Oklahoma, 1993

The EVIDENCE for Heaven

HOST **JERRY ROSE** • EXECUTIVE PRODUCERS **DON & CAROL SCIFRES**
SUPERVISING PRODUCER **CHARLES E. SELLIER**
PRODUCER **DAVID W. BALSIGER**

This docu-drama provides viewers with the testimony of 21 highly respected medical doctors, physicists, Bible scholars, authors and scientists, who have been working to prove that immortality is indeed a reality ... and that Heaven is actually more real than Earth!

Examine the facts. Reveiw the biblical findings. View the evidence. Decide for yourself if Heaven is your final destiny! Includes 50-page CD/DVD curriculum on Heaven.

To Order Your DVD/VHS
Call (800) 811-0548 toll free
www.grizzlyadams.tv